Gerald Anderson

Japanese Contributions to Christian Theology

Japanese Contributions to Christian Theology

by CARL MICHALSON

THE WESTMINSTER PRESS | PHILADELPHIA

LIBRARY OF CONGRESS CATALOG CARD NO. 60-7487

PRINTED IN THE UNITED STATES OF AMERICA

To
Edwin Lewis
and
Edwin Yoshiaki Noro

συνπολῖται

Contents

Preface 9

I The Theology of Biblical Interpretation 17
The Bible Without the Church
The Bible Within the Church

II The Theology of Church Existence 46

III The Theology of the Pain of God 73

IV The Theology of the Time of Love 100

V The Maturity of Japanese Theology 126

Notes 163

Index 185

Preface

PROTESTANT CHRISTIANITY IS ONLY ONE HUNDRED YEARS OLD in Japan. That means the Japanese Church is one of the younger churches in Christendom. Yet, of all the younger churches, it is apparently the first to have developed a significant theology. For the last twenty-five years there has been emerging among these people a theological climate that is expressing itself today in several commanding points of view. That fact is a miracle. The miracle is forced to exist in a shadow, however. How must it feel to be a first-class theological community in a world church that professes to be *one* church, knowing everything of importance that is going on in the theological world, yet itself remaining unknown? Such is the situation in which the Japanese theologians are working today. There is a language curtain that admits light from West to East, but stubbornly thwarts all theological illumination from East to West. This book is offered, therefore, as an initial attack upon such walls of ignorance now dividing the church. It is hoped that this study will breach the wall and lead the way to mutually fruitful theological conversation.

Of course, one may ask how the language barrier to

which I have referred has suddenly dissolved for me, making this work possible. How does it happen that one who is completely ignorant of the Japanese language can write a volume drawn almost exclusively from Japanese sources? During the spring semester of 1958, I was in Tokyo as the guest of Union Theological Seminary and Aoyama Gakuin University. In both these schools I was visiting lecturer in theology. To fulfill my duties I pursued what seemed the normal pedagogical path. I simply attempted to determine how much my students already knew about theology, who their regular theological professors were, and what theological sources and opinions were most influential in their thinking. As a consequence, there began a dialogue with my students and colleagues in which some very exciting theological positions were described, points of view attributed now, not to Barth, Brunner, and Bultmann, but to exotic names I had never heard and could scarcely even pronounce, names such as Uchimura, Watanabe, Kumano, Kitamori, and Hatano. Pedagogical concern gradually turned to genuine wonder at the theological insight I received, and there followed for me a disciplined process of research into the leading sources of contemporary theology in Japan.

The fact that I do not know the Japanese language, either spoken or written, seems to have been my major advantage. Missionaries and diplomats who study the language continuously for five years still doubt their capacity to do it justice in any academic way. Yet those who have behind them years in language school would lose face doing what I did. My Japanese colleagues and students, some of whom were actually bilingual from study in America and Great Britain, spent hours with me every week, translating from the major sources while I took detailed notes. The method has proved so efficient, in fact, that some wonder why scholars do not resort to it with the more manageable languages. At the end of my five months in Japan I shipped home a carefully selected library and have continued my reading project with the help of our Japanese students at Drew University. Now scarcely a week goes by that I do not receive some new theological document from Japan.

My complete dependence upon the translations of others may put in question the technical competence of this volume. Against that eventuality I have several defenses. Technical competence must occasionally take a back seat to academic fair play. If the method I have used gets a more ecumenical hearing for Japanese theology, the work should be justified. But then one ought not to underestimate the sheer academic proficiency of the conditions under which I have worked. Take, for instance, the writings of Seiichi Hatano. (In Japanese the family name is written first, and the given name second. In this book, however, I have adopted the usual Western procedure of placing the given name first.) The Japanese people themselves regard his works as untranslatable. Yet, when one considers that in order to read a single thin Hatano volume I invested three hours a week for four months under the guidance of a Japanese philosopher, there seems to have been little neglect of thoroughness and skill. In any case, it should help to know that John Gunther wrote *Inside Russia Today* without a knowledge of Russian, and that Ruth Benedict wrote her anthropological study of the Japanese people, *The Chrysanthemum and the Sword*, not only without a knowledge of Japanese but without ever setting foot in Japan.

As a consequence of my vast reliance upon others, there are a great many to whom I am indebted. Chief among them is Prof. Yoshio Noro, of Union Theological Seminary and Aoyama Gakuin University in Tokyo. He was my interpreter while I was in Japan, my tireless translator of Japanese theological works, and my constant dialogical partner. He also gave me the honor of baptizing his infant son, Yoshiaki, with the name of his and my great teacher, Edwin Lewis. The largest bulk of translation was done for me by T. Takao, a graduate student at Tokyo Union Theological Seminary, and by Jundo Uzaki, a graduate student at Drew University. Professor Ichiro Suzuki of Aoyama Gakuin University is the one who took me through Hatano's *Time and Eternity* word by word. Akira Miyazaki, a former Drew University student, now doing graduate work at the University of Tokyo, read Hatano's *Philosophy of Religion* and some related sources. Charles H. Germany and Theodore J. Kitchen, American missionaries in Japan, who are knowledgeable in Japanese, did some translating for me and shared much insight. Others both in America and in Japan who collaborated with me include Kenichi Kida, Teruo Kobayashi, Haruko Gamblin, A. Takamori, and H. Ohmiya. Masahiko Saito checked the proofs.

Drafts of the manuscript have been read and evaluated at various stages by a great number of people. Zenda Watanabe, Yoshitaka Kumano, and Kazoh Kitamori have each read and criticized the sections pertaining to their work. In addition to their valuable comments I have had the benefit of critical readings by T. T. Brumbaugh, of the Board of Missions of the Methodist Church, John H. McCombe, of the Japan Bible Society, and Randolph L. Jones and David Swain, missionaries to Japan.

I am, of course, deeply in the debt of Drew University for permitting me leave of absence for my visit to Japan, to the faculties of the several Japanese institutions that issued to me the invitation, and to the Interboard Committee for Christian Work in Japan, which helped to sponsor the trip that led to this study. I am grateful, in addition to the two schools at which I lectured regularly, to the theologians of Kwansei Gakuin University in Nishinomiya and of the Biblical Seminary in Tokyo for their hospitality and instruction during my short lectureships in each of those places. Pat Winters typed the manuscripts and helped with the proofs and indexing. I should also cite my family, who were with me in Japan and willingly sacrificed many of the joys of tourism in allowing me to pursue this unanticipated draft upon my time, and the unselfish hospitality of Lucy Dail and Pat Patterson, our hostesses at Shōtō house in Shibuya-ku, Tokyo.

The people who know a little about what is going on in the theology of Japan have tended to dismiss it as an imitation of Western theology. Even the Japanese themselves refer to their theology as a consumption and import theology, although it is usually the less creative among them who say this about the others. It is true, of course, that the Japanese are prone to acts of imitation and that they are highly skilled at it in all areas of their culture. As the Japanese philosopher Tetsuo Watsuji has said of his people, they are " the typhoon " type, who have learned to bend to every influence from the outside. During my stay in Japan, Japanese business men on their own initiative sponsored an exhibit in Tokyo in which Western products, such as watches and cameras, were placed alongside their Japanese counterparts. Viewers were challenged to decide which product had been, as they said, " pirated." It was usually impossible to tell one from the other. A friend who was attached to the aircraft industry told me that the Japanese sometimes copy American engines down to the last detail. In one instance a crack in a new engine had to be welded before it was shipped from America to Japan. When the Japanese began production on that pirated model, they reduplicated the model right down to the weld.

Even the cracks in the Western theologies appear in their Japanese reproductions. The Japanese theologians take different attitudes toward their imitative ways, however. Some feel that in a country in which Christianity is still so new, theologians must be as faithful to the Christian tradition as possible in order to keep the faith free from syncretism. Others feel that a faith is nothing unless it becomes one's own, and that when it does become one's own it will surely reflect the traits of its bearers. Both positions might have been taken by the apostle Paul, and both will be apparent in the theologies delineated here.

Westerners ought not to be smug about the imitative tendency, however. Among American theologians, at any rate, it is commonly known that the best way to become a creative theologian is to learn to read German! I think I am not wrong in observing that the chief difference between Americans and Japanese in this regard is that Americans have found more ways of disguising their sources. That is not said to be snide. In the very process of folding the insights of others into one's own language, something creative occurs. For even where imitation prevails, selectivity and translation are required. To see a younger church choosing one trend in Christendom and rejecting another, and to discern the rationale behind that selection, is in itself an exhilarating and instructive theological experience. Moreover, to see the subtle translation of Western Christianity into the medium of Japanese is to witness what might even be creativity parallel to the generally acknowledged creativity that has occurred in Japanese art in its translation from the art of China.

No one of us interested and involved in this project can

anticipate what effect it will have, although the students at Drew now joke about how soon the Japanese language will be a prerequisite for graduate work in theology. It is hoped, however, that this brief introduction to a theology in a hitherto untapped language will pique the curiosity of Western Christendom. When allusions little by little are made to these theologians in Western discourse, when now and then a place is given to the Japanese alongside Continental theologians in discussions of contemporary theology, and when acknowledgments of Japanese works begin occasionally to appear in Western journals, the arrival of two authentic moments will thereby be heralded. The Japanese Christians will be able to affirm their belief in " one church " with new zest. More significantly, the Western Church will begin to realize toward the East what is still largely true in the abstract only, that with them we are *συνπολῖται*, " fellow citizens."

CARL MICHALSON

Drew Forest
Madison, N.J.

I The Theology of Biblical Interpretation

JAPANESE CHRISTIANS ARE A BIBLE-READING PEOPLE. A preacher who begins a sermon in Japan without announcing a text could embarrass himself, for the people in the congregation sit with their Bibles poised. When the Bible first came to Japan it seemed like a very Western book because it came in European and English translations and was received from the white, hairy hands of Westerners. The Japanese have long since discovered, however, that the Bible is really an Oriental book. The story of Moses in the presence of the burning bush reads like a page out of Japanese history when you hear the text, " Put off thy *geta* from off thy feet, for the place whereon thou standest is holy ground." It has been said by Takeshi Fujii, one of the patriarchs of the Non-Church movement, that Japanese children understand the Bible even *better* than they understand their own national history. Therefore, " to regard the Bible as a book for Westerners only is the shame of the Oriental." [1]

The larger question about the place of the Bible in Japanese theological thinking is not how a Japanese can assimilate a Semitic book. It is whether the Japanese, by virtue of their long history of cultural isolation, may not have a very unique role to play in conserving a pure form of Biblical Christianity for the rest of Christendom. Just because they have remained so long untinctured by Westernism, into whose forms the Biblical faith has been pressed, may they not be a people with a mission to restore Biblical Christianity more nearly to its primitive intention? The founder of the Non-Church movement, Kanzō Uchimura, once had a dream to that effect. He saw a heavy dew falling upon Mount Fuji. It was the dew of divine grace. The waters of the dew flowed to the east and to the west until the whole world was covered with its divine purity. When he awakened he said, " *Amen*, so let it be." He interpreted the dream as a prophecy of Japan's role in world Christendom. A pure form of Biblical Christianity that would rejuvenate all Christendom was to spring from Japan. Non-Church Christianity is the concrete form that his vision has taken in Japan today.

The Bible Without the Church

The distinctive thing about *Mukyōkai*, or Non-Church Christianity, is its effort to participate in the Christian faith without the church. Its method of achieving this goal is found in adherence to the Bible alone, which means to the Bible as a book that is read in deliberate independence of the organized life of the church.

A definition of " Non-Church " is difficult to determine, for the very connotation of structure and norm required in a definition is alien to the spirit of Non-Church. There are a variety of definitions, however. All participate in some form of denial of ecclesiasticism as it has appeared in Western Christianity. The only difference among them is in the vehemence of the denial. Some denials are benign; others brand the ecclesiastical religionists as satanic. W. H. H.

Norman's definition seems most universally acceptable. Non-Church, he has said, " should include any group of people, unconnected with a church, who study the Bible and Christianity." [2] From that standpoint, the prefix, *mu-*, is misleading. For *mu-* denotes positive negation or annihilation. As *kyōkai* means " church," *mu-kyōkai* would mean the movement that " annihilates the church." Uchimura early attempted to dispel that supposition. In the very first issue of his magazine, *Mukyōkai*, in March of 1910 he proposed the Japanese prefix *nai-* as an alternative to *mu-*, for *nai-* means simply " nonexisting." Non-Church, he claimed, " is the church for people who do not have a church." Therefore, as he said, it is the spiritual equivalent of an orphanage.

Mukyōkai seems to be destructive, but it is really constructive. It seems to be awesome, but it is really meek. It seems to wear the skin of a bear, but really has the heart of a lamb. It seems to be urging reform and revolt in society, yet it desires to befriend small girls and old people. We may seem to wear the mask of *Hannja* [a demon famous in Japan for its fearful face], but our main interest is to threaten those who pay attention only to exterior things in order to help them see the interior things.[3]

The intention of *Mukyōkai*, so far as it can be uniformly described, is to achieve a pure Christianity that " loves God and man without the church." It may surprise some to know that one of Uchimura's early inspirations for this movement away from churchism was Sören Kierkegaard. Kierkegaard reportedly had said he had never seen a genuine Christian in this world. Uchimura did not conclude from this that Christianity was false or that he could not be a Christian. Even though there were no Christians in Japan, he decided he could be the first. Hence, he set about to be a Christian in a way the church had not yet tried, namely, without the church. At the death of Tolstoy, upon hearing that Tolstoy had prearranged not to have his service in the church, Uchimura exclaimed, "Bless his heart, he too died by refusing the comfort of the pastor and the church, just as Sören Kierkegaard did."

If Christians around the world know anything about Japanese theology, it is usually related to the Non-Church movement. This knowledge is generally traceable to Emil Brunner's appreciative estimate to the effect that Non-Church Christianity is "a purely Japanese type of Christianity which truly meets and understands the Japanese spirit." What Brunner finds to be its asset, some may hold to be its liability. Is not this form of Christianity a Japanese distortion brought on by an excessively nationalistic spirit? Can it be attributed solely to homesickness that Uchimura wrote from the United States in 1885, "Those sweetest of names – Christ and Japan!" and that he signed the same letter, "Yours in Christ and Japan"? Is it of merely theological interest that the famous political scientist and one-time president of Tokyo University, Tadao Yanaibara, likens the Non-Church reformation in Japan to Luther's Reformation, calling attention to the fact that with the Reformation came Luther's call for the independence of the German people, their religious and their political freedom, and that Luther regarded the Germans as a chosen race? [4]

There is no disputing the nationalism in the Non-Church movement, just as there is no disputing the methodism in the Wesleyan revival. *Mukyōkai* adherents are called "cross-legged" Christians as the Wesleys were called "methodists," in derision. Instead of sitting in Western-churches on Western-style pews, listening to Western-style sermons preached by missionaries and pastors supported by Western money, they sit cross-legged on straw mats in homes, factories, schools, and anywhere — except Churches — studying the Bible. There is no church edifice, no clergy, no sacraments, no organization. Only the Bible is read and interpreted, and no one has any more authority than anyone else in the act of interpretation. There are real grounds for observing that Christianity has taken this form for a great body of Japanese who desire to be Christian without ceasing to be Japanese, or without capitulating to a non-Japanese way of life under the illusion that it is thereby a Christian way of life. In the Meiji era, when Christianity was widely accepted for cultural reasons, Christians in Japan were called " butter-stinking " people. Only Americans ate butter in Japan, and the Christians were " America lovers." Why is it not a sign of authenticity, then, that the Non-Church Christians sense their faith emanating from the dew of grace with which God in his providence adorns Japan in some original sense?

The inscription on the tomb of Uchimura symbolizes a transcendence of nationalism in the direction of Christian responsibility:

> I for Japan
> Japan for the world
> The world for Christ
> And all for God.

It may be taken as a sign of maturity and not of inconsistency that the inscription is in English. For instance, the Non-Church Christians, along with the Holiness groups, were the Christians most conspicuous in their resistance to the imperialistic drift of the Government in the war years.

Yanaibara was dismissed from his position as a professor in the University of Tokyo for his criticism of the Japanese policies in Formosa, Manchuria, and Korea, and for calling upon the Government to make itself as nothing before the world as its sole hope for deliverance from catastrophe. Fifty years earlier in a similar posture Uchimura was dismissed from his position in a state-supported school for refusing to kneel before the picture of the emperor when the imperial rescript was read. The charge of nationalism scarcely holds up under the evidence of Non-Church behavior toward the governments of Japan. Nor is the animus of the movement directed simply against governments. Fujii, the angry young man of Non-Churchism, once wrote a poem about his homeland with the rather unreserved title "Be destroyed!"

Is Japan rising or falling?
Is she blessed or accursed?
. . . . . .
One night last summer I overheard
A conversation between some young people,
And I trembled.
Early the next morning I fled like Lot fleeing Sodom.
Since then, I cannot escape the premonition of the fall of Japan.
Before long this kind of country will be destroyed,
This land of defiled girls and degenerate youth.
. . . . . .
I would agree in hot tears with the dying words of my teacher
    Uchimura:
"Tell them I have left this kind of country
With no regrets."
Woe to a people which continually rebels against the truth —
    this country.
O Lord, thy will be done.[5]

To attempt to explain Non-Church Christianity without patient theological analysis would be irresponsible. In a recent statement on how to read theology, one of the theologians of the United Church of Japan (*Kyōdan*) observed that one should look for two things: the attitude toward the church and the attitude toward the Bible.[6] In Non-Church Christianity the doctrines of church and Bible not only supply the clue to its theology; they *are* its theology. The treatment of even these doctrines, however, displays a form of reductionism in which the religious significance of the church is shrunk to the point where only the Bible is left as the source of Christian existence.

The church that the movement repudiates is not necessarily the church that it finds in the Bible. It is rather the established church, that is, the objective institution that has guaranteed its own historical continuity by acts of exclusiveness and self-perpetuation. Jesus announced the coming of the Kingdom of God, and the church appeared. In the failure of the Kingdom to come as announced, the church attempted to justify itself as complete in itself. This deviation from the intention of Jesus has lasted two thousand years and shows up in Japan today in the form of ecclesiastical exclusiveness. As Sekine has said, "In Japan today the church has walls around it."[7]

What, then, is the true form that Christianity should take, the form that Non-Church Christianity believes it manifests? Non-Church understands itself as an "assembly of Christians," a "congregation of believers filled with the spirit" (Yanaibara). It is "the gathering of the saved" (Sekine), the "*koinōnia* with God and Christ," "the living organism of all in fellowship with God" (Kurosaki).

By these definitions the Non-Church group does not reject entirely the concept of a church. The Christian movement must always take some form. As Uchimura was fond of saying, " Non-Church must progress toward having a church." Nor is Non-Church particularly critical of the form the church has taken in the past. Some concede that the church of the past adequately fulfilled its role for its day, which was to evangelize. But when the forms the church has taken in the past become the forms of the present church simply by blind inertia, and when these forms thwart the evangelical purposes of the faith, Non-Church arises in judgment to create openness toward the proper shape of the church.

The objective institutionalism of the present-day, Westernized church is considered by the Non-Church group to be " a petrified reality " in which the spirit of God cannot easily work. The visible church must remember it is only a medium for the invisible. The church is a body of believers first, an objective reality second. But there is no adequate mark in its objectivity by which Christians can be distinguished from the world. And there is no way in which the church, being an organism, can reproduce itself. " Since Non-Church is not an institution, it is more personal, dynamic, and historical. By rejecting petrified forms, we create new, living forms." [8] In the Bible, " we can find no idea of institution, of legal authority and offices, or of definite sacramentalism, at least not as of central importance. All the apostles taught *koinōnia* with God and with men in loving unity with Jesus Christ." [9]

One manifestation of an undesirable objectivity in the church is the role played by rites, sacraments, and creeds. Again, the attitude among Non-Church adherents varies all the way from rejection to toleration. According to Kōkichi Kurosaki, a professional Bible scholar, " the apostles did not think that Christ had instituted Baptism and the Lord's Supper as sacramental rites. . . . Neither did the apostles establish any creeds or doctrines." [10] A somewhat softer point of view is expressed by Masao Sekine who believes that "even though Christ himself commanded Baptism and the Lord's Supper, we need not conclude that we should practice the rituals as they have become established." [11] That is to say, the form in which these rites have reached the church today bears no resemblance to what Jesus had in mind when he instituted them. Least of all was it intended that these rites be turned into devices for exclusion. As Sekine comments, the Non-Church group has often observed the sacraments. It is not said that they are meaningless. When they are correctly used, they offer the essence of the gospel visibly and provide an occasion for fellowship. They are only wrong if one looks on them as objective, regarding them as indispensable for salvation. That attitude does not correspond to the truth that we are saved by faith.[12] Even though Jesus may have commanded the sacraments, his greatest commandment is to love God and men. "All other commandments are secondary." [13]

Two major questions continually confront the Non-Church movement from the side of church groups. The answers to both these questions bear directly upon the prominence that the Bible plays in Non-Church Christianity.

First, do Non-Church Christians desire to re-enact in the twentieth century the primitive, Biblical description of Christian life? In a certain sense, yes. "The true pattern of Christianity is to be found in the first-century catacombs, where there were no ecclesiastical regulations and rituals and where Christians could praise God with their heart and life." [14] In another sense, however, "our problem is how we should understand church history." [15] Are not all churches, including the primitive church, made by men?

That would mean there is no perfect church. It would be meaningless, for instance, to attempt to reduplicate the church of Paul after two thousand years. There is no continuity of the church within history because the fact that founds the church is the resurrection of Christ, which is not an intrahistorical reality. If the church is founded from beyond history, then in every moment Christians must maintain the attitude that makes it possible for the church to be born anew in their time.[16] On that basis, the Non-Church movement does not go back to primitive Christianity but only to the spirit that gave rise to it.

For the same reason, Non-Churchism dissociates itself from the Protestant Reformation. Luther " did not complete his work of Reformation because he maintained the church system with its sacraments." [17] Although Uchimura is listed as a reformer alongside Jeremiah, Jesus, Paul, and Luther, he is believed to have gone beyond Luther's idea of the church. Luther kept the ministry under the authority of the organized church. He failed to hold the tension in which the preacher is a mere believer and yet has spiritual authority.[18] Therefore, Non-Churchism claims to be a thoroughgoing advance beyond Protestantism. The Non-Church movement is believed to be the greatest, so far as reformer types are concerned, because the Protestant Reformers cut nothing away, but Non-Church cuts away the church in its traditional form. Non-Church is therefore regarded as a third and independent ground alongside Roman Catholicism and Protestantism, and as the " true and final form of Christianity." [19]

The second question directed at the Non-Church movement is, What keeps you from falling off into chaos without becoming another church? The answer some give is that, naturally, a group of Christians gathered today continues to come together tomorrow. It does not vitiate itself miscellaneously. But it comes together tomorrow not for the sheer fact that it came together yesterday but for the same reason.[20] That answer seems a bit idealistic. Indeed, the main criticism of the Non-Church movement has to do with the way it overspiritualizes the church, its followers attempting to exist as Christians in a community and in history without conceding the essential embodiment connoted by historical community. However, the Non-Church group is simply amused by this sort of criticism directed against them by present-day Protestants, for it is the precise criticism that was once directed against Protestants by Roman Catholicism.[21]

The reason the answer seems idealistic, however, is that there are excellent non-spiritual factors to account for the mobility and coherence of the Non-Church group, factors that participate in peculiarly Oriental traits. Saburō Takahashi suggests this when he calls attention to the way Confucian teachers drew large groups of students around them with no organization to support them, yet with such power that even feudal lords sought them out for instruction instead of requiring the teachers to come to them. Then, citing Uchimura, who once said, " It is much nobler to follow Confucian teachers than to follow missionaries," he comments, we are " sanctified Confucian teachers." [22] The strong role that outstanding Bible teachers, such as Uchimura, Fujii, Yanaibara, Kurosaki, and others, have played in the short history of *Mukyōkai* surely testifies to the way a group can stay together without calculated organization. Uchimura once limited his Bible classes to twenty members and required one year's reading of his monthly magazine, *Biblical Studies,* in advance of entrance to his class. Yanaibara recalls the date of his admission to Uchimura's class with the same fondness with which evangelical Christians recall the date of their conversion. Fujii's testimony is also typical. One day in the fall of 1909 a friend invited him to visit the city in which Uchimura was teaching. " Won't you try to visit our teacher? " he said. " He is looking for more students." Fujii decided to go, as he confessed, " for the teacher's sake."

> That night Uchimura talked about enduring persecution for the sake of faith. As I listened to him, my heart burned strangely. After a few days I made my decision and asked to become a disciple of that teacher. Uchimura was the only one I ever called teacher in that sense. Indeed, he was a prophet pointing to Christ.[23]

Has the Bible teacher, then, become the same kind of cohesive factor in Oriental Christianity that the bishop came to be in the land of the imperator? If that were in any sense so, there would be one main difference. In *Mukyōkai* the rectorial role of the teacher is uncalculated. Or even if it were in some instances calculated, no rationale is adduced to support the role.

The genuine, calculated, and theologically avowed center of cohesion in this group is the Bible itself, and only the Bible. In an opinion poll recently conducted by W. H. H. Norman among a representative body of Christians from all the churches of Japan, the main influence of Uchimura upon them was said to be his reverence for and knowledge and understanding of the Bible.[24] This is true, notwithstanding the fact that theories about the nature of the Bible by Non-Church spokesmen fill a spectrum that ranges all the way from verbal inspiration to the policies of the most scientific literary criticism.

One may conclude from this that the Non-Church movement is bound to the Bible in practice, irrespective of theories about the Bible. The Bible is the criterion for faith. A most beautiful statement of the indispensability of the Bible was made by Fujii in 1921. In an article entitled " If there had been no Bible . . . ? " he confesses quite frankly that the Bible is not at all indispensable if it is there simply to satisfy the human aspiration for religion, or as support for the moral life, or as wisdom for a comfortable life in the world. The questions of religion, morality, philosophy, science, literature, art, and law are not the questions to which the Bible speaks. " If our questions are raised simply in regard to our happiness or our understanding of the meaning of life, the Bible must be said to be a useless book. Indeed, it is not only useless but harmful. . . . I would even dare to venture that the Bible does not generally promote the so-called happiness of this world. It destroys it." [25]

Without the Bible, however, man would live in ignorance concerning four major elements in the purpose of human life. The Bible first of all tells us who God is, the Holy Father who has condescended to come among us in Jesus Christ for the sake of sinners. Second, it tells us who man is in his true nature, created according to the image of God, with infinite dignity and worth, yet corrupted by rebelliousness toward God and affected by the desperate consequences of that rebellion. Third, it gives us an understanding of the environment that surrounds us, which we call nature. According to the Bible, nature originates in " the most beautiful impulse of love." Its supreme axiom, therefore, is not to be found in physical laws but in the notion of the Creator himself. Yet because the man who was created in God's image has nevertheless revolted against God, nature as man's environment suffers the calamities which that rebellion inaugurates. Finally, without the Bible, mankind would live out its life ignorant of the solution of its predicament. Therefore, " the ultimate purpose of the Bible exists in the revelation of man's salvation." Salvation is to be understood entirely as a matter of grace. " Without any compulsion from the outside or any necessity, but purely out of the impulse of his love, God seeks to save those whom there is no reason to save." [26] The incarnation of God in his Son Jesus Christ was the preparation for this salvation, and the truth of what God has prepared in Christ is communicated in the Bible.

Giving the Bible practical primacy in their lives is the Non-Church movement's way of avoiding what would be for them the inconsistency of adopting the Bible as the canon of the church. Although the Christian is bound to the Bible, he is not believed to be bound to it under the authority of the church. It was long after the writings of the apostles and the sayings of Jesus became authoritative for Christians that the church created the authoritative canon we now know as our Bible. Therefore, the Christian movement need not be thought to be dependent upon the church for the authority of the Biblical faith. Indeed, there is ample Biblical evidence to show that Jesus and Paul were both opposed to the principle of canonicity, that is, to conferring final authority upon some documentary witness to faith. Jesus and his disciples opposed the legalistic principle of canonicity that was employed by the Jews. He stood against the Pharisees' interpretation of the law (e.g., Matt. 5:21). He made friends with the illiterate (John 7:49) and with sinners, even though it was contrary to the custom of the Pharisees (Mark 2:17). This is taken to be a sign of Jesus' protest against the characteristics of a formalistic religion, especially with its tendency to center in a canon. Paul protested against a religion of letter on behalf of a religion of spirit (Rom., ch. 7) and actually fought formal canonicity (Phil. 3:5-7). In fact, according to the New Testament scholar, Gorō Maeda, of the University of Tokyo, it is this very freedom of Christianity from canonicity which separates it from religions of the book such as Mohammedanism, Manichaeanism, and Judaism.[27] In the history of Christianity, he says, many evangelicals such as Augustine and Luther respected the Bible, but not as a formal canon. Eventually, after the Reformation and the Counter Reformation, all Christendom began to read the Bible, not simply in the church, but in the home.

When the Non-Church movement reads the Bible outside the church, how does it avoid the excesses implicit in private interpretation? There are two kinds of answer to that question. On the one hand, liberation from canonicity has set the Christian scholars free for the scientific study of the Bible. The most sharply trained and rigorous philologists and historical critics in Japanese Christianity are in the Non-Church group. The Bible is an aggregate of a great many books written from a great many points of view. " It is the privilege and responsibility of the Bible reader to enter into the world of the early Christian by a scientific analysis of the Bible as literature, free from the standpoint of the Bible as canon." [28] This can be done, it is felt, with no jeopardy to the believer's finding the center of his spiritual life in the Bible. The truth of that is evident in the fact that Jesus himself criticized the complicated " human traditions " of the Pharisees, not to be destructive, but to open the way for the true commandment of God in the Bible (Mark 7:1-13). Paul explained that his conversion to Christianity was related to his emancipation from the " traditions of my ancestors," as the Japanese version of the letter states it (Gal. 1:14). The New Testament, which teaches the gospel of freedom from limitless rules and mere religious observance, reveals the mystery of God's boundless grace precisely in its freedom from canonicity.[29]

The other answer by the Non-Church group to the fear of private interpretation is in the claim of the movement that their interpretation of the Bible is not individual. "We read it as a group."[30] What that means in practice may differ from group to group. In theory, however, the simple rejection of the church in its traditional form does not necessarily connote sectarian individualism for the Non-Church movement. Fujii explained this as early as 1925. The church is rejected as a means to the salvation of the individual, he said. The church in its true sense is not a flock of sheep or an organization of people who believe. "The church is in itself a unitary, single person." Indeed, if the church is not simply the bride of Christ but the body of Christ, it cannot even be looked upon as an independent reality alongside Christ. For this reason, individualism is believed to be an enemy of Christian life,[31] and the reading of the Bible is a community responsibility in which there is no authority but Christ.

Now, the Bible is an objectively embodied, concretely organized body of literature. The Non-Church group places this book at the very center of its spiritual existence. How do they avoid the charge that in supplanting the church by the Bible they have adopted the Bible as their "paper pope"? The theoretical denials that this has been the case are legion. The practical evidences tell a different story. Since the foundation of the movement, people who claim they are freethinkers have used the Bible as if it were verbally infallible. Fujii was one of these. He once said, "The Almighty is the author of this book. Hence nothing can be added or subtracted." Even Uchimura's use of the Bible was often literalistic, so that he tended to be caught by the surface meaning of texts, giving his exegesis the appearance of dogmatism.[32]

From a theoretical standpoint, Sekine's account of the nature of the Bible is a most instructive clue to the more enlightened Non-Church attitude today. He himself introduces the question as to why the Non-Church group can depend upon the Bible as they do, considering that the Bible is as ready-made as the church that they reject. Obviously the answer cannot be, Because the church has canonized it. "The past does not bind us." The answer is that the Bible is the authoritative book because it leads to the revelation, to the living Christ who alone binds us.[33] And how does one get the living, resurrected Christ from the dead Word? He does so neither by an objective, literalistic approach to the text, nor by a subjectivistic (*shukanteki*), private interpretation. He grasps the Bible subjectively (*shutaiteki*). That is, the deep, divine, spiritual unity that animates the Biblical witness is allowed to witness to itself.[34] When Bible-reading is pursued on that basis, the exalted Christ becomes the Lord of life.

One of the fascinating things about studying theology in a foreign language is the shade of meaning communicated through linguistic distinctions. The Japanese language is an enormously versatile theological language. Where other languages have one word for an ambiguous concept, the Japanese often have two words, thus overcoming the ambiguity. One cannot say "subjective" in English, for instance, without equivocation. "Subjective" can mean a state of private feeling, as in most popular speech; or it can mean an intimate personal encounter with a reality outside oneself, an encounter that contributes wholeness to the person. This is its meaning in contemporary existential thinking. For the former, the Japanese use the word *shukan-teki*, for the latter, *shutaiteki*. The suffix, *-teki*, converts the nouns, *shukan* and *shutai*, meaning " subject," into adjectives, " subjective." *Shutai-sei* and *shukan-sei* mean " subjectivity." Martin Heidegger, the German existentialist, has recently invented a verbal distinction that serves the same purpose. The German term *Subjektivität* was always subject to the same equivocation as its English equivalent " subjectivity." Therefore, *Subjektität* was created to bear the special meaning that the Japanese *shutai-sei* connotes. It is translated " subjecticity."

Like their founder, Uchimura, the Non-Church " theologians " are primarily " lay Biblical evangelists." Uchimura applied that title to himself in an article he entitled " I hate theology! " It is obvious, however, that the very practice of the Non-Church group is suffused with theological implications, and at the two points where theology is most pivotal for the Japanese, the doctrine of the church and the doctrine of the Bible. It is also obvious that Non-Churchism is succeeding as a judgment upon the inadequacies of the life of the church. The counterthrust of the theologians of the church, however, ought not be written off as mere ecclesiastical defensiveness. Non-Churchism not only puts the Bible at the center but makes it the exclusive source of the Christian life. Can the Bible really be adequately understood unless it is interpreted from within the church? That question, the counterproposal of the major theologians of Japan, opens up one of the most fruitful conversations in Japanese theology today.

The Bible Within the Church

The theologian most directly involved with the question of the locus for the interpretation of the Bible is Zenda

Watanabe, a theologian of the United Church of Christ in Japan (*Nihon Kirisuto Kyōdan*). One of the major theological events in Japan during the present decade has been the appearance of his prodigious two-volume work on *The Doctrine of the Scriptures*. The work merits attention for its own sake, consummating as it does a mature Old Testament scholar's lifelong preoccupation with the method of Biblical interpretation. His contribution takes on special theological importance for Japanese Christians, however, in the way it emphasizes the place of the church in the interpretation of the Bible. As has been seen, Non-Church Christians pursue the conviction that they can be Christians without the church, simply by a faithful study of the Bible. Zenda Watanabe, with no thought of polemics, has developed the position that there is no faithful study of the Bible, that is, no study of the Bible as the word of God, that does not occur within the framework of the church.

The Bible is comprised of sixty-six different books and almost as many authors. According to Watanabe, that fact is misleading, for the Bible has been assembled as one book by the Christian church, officially in the fourth century. At that time the Church canonized the Scriptures. In doing so, it overcame the problem of the diversity of Biblical authorship and shifted the center of interpretational concern. Now that the church has acknowledged the Bible as authority in faith and life, the interpreter no longer simply asks who the author was and what the author meant when he originally wrote the text. The interpreter also asks what the church meant when it canonized the text. Therefore, interpretation of the Bible as the word of God involves participation in the faith of the historical church that created the Bible as canon. Against the background of that understanding, Watanabe has developed his theory of the interpretation of the Bible as the canon of the church. The theory is proposed as an advance upon the three major hermeneutical methods that have dominated Biblical studies in the history of Christianity. As I see it, its theological importance is its challenge to the main premise of the Non-Church movement.

The three methods in the history of hermeneutics, all of which are judged to be inadequate, are the allegorical, the dogmatic, and the historical. The *allegorical method*, which developed in Alexandria, has the weakness of supplanting the work of the Holy Spirit in the process of interpretation. The method radically reinterprets texts whose evident meaning has been subjected to doubt. By allegorizing the text, it invents meanings that were not originally intended in the text but that nevertheless seem plausible. The *dogmatic method* has the weakness of giving church tradition priority over the Biblical text. Where the Bible does not seem to confirm tradition, the Bible is presumed to lack value and meaning. As Hugh of St. Victor claimed, one must first learn what it is necessary to believe, *then* go to the Bible. The church becomes the premise for faith in the Bible. The plausibility of this method is patent: the Bible being frequently ambiguous, it needs some criterion by which the interpreter can resolve its ambiguities. The dogmatic method locates that criterion in the theological decisions of the church. This was the point of view against which the Protestant Reformers had to contend. In the process, they made new beginnings in Biblical interpretation that were meant to give the Bible priority over the tradition of the church. However, all attempts in this direction were immediately exaggerated by orthodox Protestantism into some version of verbal inspiration that encouraged the practice of proof-texting and confessionalism. The third method of interpretation is the *historical method*. It began as early as Diodorus of Tarsus, was continued by Theodore of Mopsuestia, and has become the dominant method in modern academic circles. Its basic presupposition is that there must be no presupposition. The facts must be allowed to speak for themselves. The claim to presuppositionlessness is the major fallacy of this position.[35]

Watanabe contends that in the meantime "the Protestant church has not developed a satisfactory theory of the interpretation of the Scriptures." [36] The story of how he himself came to sense this lack reveals a life of impressive simplicity and sensitivity. Early in his experience he attended a class that Uchimura was teaching. The text under consideration was I Cor. 15:51, concerned with the return of Christ. Uchimura made the statement that Paul could have said what he did about Christ's purported Second Coming only because he knew nothing about Darwin's evolutionary hypothesis. In these days, he said, nobody believes in this verse. Watanabe became very angry with the teacher, for he strongly believed in the Second Coming of Christ, convinced as he was of the infallibility of the Scriptures. Persuaded that Uchimura's interpretation was an act of spiritual cowardice, Watanabe spoke up with reference to the verse in question. "I believe it is true," he said, "and that what the Bible says will happen exactly as it is written." Uchimura replied, "That shows how ignorant you are." [37]

Watanabe's initial contacts with Christianity had been through the Holiness group, which based its teachings upon some emphases in the thought of John Wesley. The method of Biblical interpretation in this group was to search for anything in the Scriptures that would confirm sanctification by the Holy Spirit and holiness of life as the prerequisite for salvation. Watanabe records in his autobiography the great shock he experienced in being confronted by another group that had a different understanding of Christianity based upon the same Bible. The Plymouth Brethren read the Bible from an entirely different doctrinal prejudice, the Second Coming of Christ and the restoration of Israel. Where the Plymouth Brethren interpreters referred to Old Testament texts as prophecies of the restoration of Israel, the Holiness interpreters found in them the divine requirement for holiness of life. A familiar instance is Ezek. 36:25-27. Now both the Plymouth Brethren and the Wesleyans had faith in God and believed in the Bible as the word of God. Why, then, did they understand the Bible in different ways? Watanabe's response to the threat of this antimony was not to ask, " Which of these two views is right? " Rather, with characteristic Oriental judiciousness he asked, " How *should* the Bible be interpreted? " This " academic challenge " became the problem of his entire life. Although he continued to preach, his heart was not in it. He had now come to feel that it was his mission in life to find an answer to the hermeneutical question.[38]

The opportunity arose through the Holiness group for Watanabe to study in America. After a short term in a Nazarene school, he transferred to the Pacific School of Religion. There he was fully trained in the historical method of interpretation. With these scientific tools of Biblical study he returned to Japan, the first Old Testament scholar to apply to the Bible the methodology of historical criticism. No more forcing upon the Bible dogmatic presuppositions that were alien to it. The Bible must be allowed to speak for itself, as any other book in the history of literature does. What seemed to satisfy the majority of Christian interpreters at this time, however, did not quite satisfy Watanabe. That realization came to him under the most modest circumstances. A student once asked him with evident seriousness if there were not some way of understanding the Bible and becoming a Christian without the use of the elaborate technical skills of historical criticism. Watanabe, with a heavy professional investment in technical skills, was stunned by the inferences in so simple and pious a question. The question became the occasion for his leaving Japan again to pursue his quest for a proper method of interpretation, this time in Germany, where he entered into the hermeneutical emphases that Wilhelm Dilthey, Edmund Husserl, and Martin Heidegger had developed. What resulted was a strengthening of his conviction that a proper understanding of theology is based upon a proper understanding of the Bible, making the question of Biblical interpretation a very serious theological problem. The aspect of this result that is most significant for the contemporary theological scene in Japan is his development of the theory of the interpretation of the Scriptures as the canon of the church.

In Watanabe's fully developed position there are four emphases that relate to the place of the church in understanding the Bible. First, the theological interpretation of the Bible must have primacy over historical criticism. This position has long been in force in contemporary theology, largely through the influence of the dialectical theology, beginning with Karl Barth's commentary on Paul's letter to the Romans. Watanabe, however, has attempted to formulate the position with greater rigor. The position is based upon the assumption that there is a difference between the Bible and literature in general. For Christians, the Bible is the rule of faith and life. That is the meaning of the church's canonization of the Bible. Therefore, one who interprets the Bible cannot act as if he is approaching it without presuppositions, and one cannot suppose that he is getting its message when he is asking simply the objective and technical questions, such as those having to do with the date and authorship of the documents involved. One cannot ask simply how the Bible was made. He must ask what it is. When he does, three dimensions of hermeneutic responsibility, and not just one, claim him. He needs to know not merely what the author meant by the writing in the first place. He needs also to know what the church meant by canonizing it, and what the document therefore means to us in the present. That is, the Bible has two natures. It is a literature, which has an author, and it is a canon, which presupposes an editor, the church. When it confronts the interpreter, a third dimension is added to its nature: its relevance to the interpreter.[39] In respect of this third aspect, the Bible reconstructs itself within the interpreter, making his subjectivity (*shutai-sei*) its medium.[40]

Christians who treat the Bible as a reference book (*sankō*) rather than as a rule of faith and life (*kijun*) will misunderstand their faith. At the same time, when Christians are faithful to the Bible (*seisho*) as canon (*seiten*), as the Reformers were in their dispute with the Roman Church, they are in a position to regain the authentic form of the church. Roman Catholicism corrupted the Christian faith by allowing tradition (*denshō*) to become a standard (*kijun*) coordinate with the Bible. The rationalists of the eighteenth century corrupted the faith by treating the Bible simply as a reference book (*sankō*), without consideration of its status as rule of faith (*kijun*). To treat the Bible as a reference book is the same mistake as to treat it as one of two coordinate forms of authoritative tradition. In both cases the Bible is required to surrender its initiative to sources of interpretation outside the Bible.[41]

The second emphasis in Watanabe's theory has to do with the way the Bible asserts itself in the moment it is being interpreted. Canonicity is not appealed to by Watanabe as the cause of the Bible's authority. Canonicity is the church's recognition of the self-assertion of the Bible as the rule of faith and life. The Bible, therefore, resists the objective treatment that historical interpretation has attempted to employ. Drawing upon the categories of Martin Buber, Watanabe says the Bible does not respond to approaches that are appropriate for an " it " form of reality. The Bible asserts itself in living confrontation as if it were a " thou." The church, then, does not claim the Bible to be the authority; it simply claims that the Bible is a book that puts an authoritative claim upon the church. That is why, to say it as one of Watanabe's disciples does, " the Bible outranks the church." [42] Just as those who construct a constitution for their country stand under the authority of the constitution notwithstanding the fact that it is they who have created it, so the church that has composed the Bible stands under its authority.

In the third place, in Watanabe's view the very location of the books of the Bible within the canon affects the interpretation of the Bible. The rather debatable claim is made by Miss Okamura that one cannot find the self-assertion of the Bible in any single book of the Bible.[43] The meaning of that claim, however, is that the Bible is a *Gestalt*, a structure of books, which depends for its impact in a measure upon the appropriation of the Bible as a whole. To say that no single book lays a claim upon the interpreter would be to overlook such evangelical experiences as reported of Augustine, Luther, and Wesley where the Bible became a closed book but for a single writing, or chapter, or even verse. The wholeness of the Bible can be manifested in a single verse, without reference to the whole of the Bible. That kind of experience, however, ought not be taken as normative for exegetical responsibility. Even such cataclysmic illuminations from isolated passages must eventually be held responsible to the whole of the Bible.

The question of the whole Bible involves the question of the strategy of the church in arranging the books of the Bible in the form in which they have been given to the church. Here the differences, oppositions, and contradictions within the literature are frankly acknowledged and turned to hermeneutical advantage. It is not necessary to agree in detail with Watanabe's conclusions from this claim in order to agree with his general method. One of his conclusions is that the very structure of the New Testament supports the understanding that Christ is the center of history. The Gospels testify to Christ's impact upon the past; the epistles to his impact upon the present; and the book of the Revelation to his impact upon the future. The Old Testament also divides into three parts. The priestly literature emphasizes the law that demands that we understand correct worship. In that sense it is a witness to Jesus Christ. The prophetic literature speaks now of judgment and fall, now of the coming of the Messiah. These apparently divergent testimonies must not be separated. Taken together they convey the meaning that the faithful will prosper and the unfaithful will perish. The wisdom literature has the purpose of arousing God-given wisdom in the heart. Ecclesiastes, for instance, takes the position that logical search for ultimate meaning is vain – one must stand within the faith in God – or that by worldly wisdom the people of God can be diverted from the true object of their love. Wisdom, however, will lead Israel to a genuine understanding of love. In this sense, wisdom leads to Christ, who is greater than Solomon (Matt. 12:42).[44]

Another way of interpreting the same threefold division

of the Old Testament suggests that the Torah establishes the existence of Israel as God's chosen people. The prophetic literature is a warning to Israel of its default in its mission as a people and a prediction of forthcoming catastrophe. The wisdom literature describes what Israel has been and what Israel has failed to be. What can one conclude hermeneutically from the structure between these three bodies of literature? "This structure in the three divisions of the Old Testament indicates, however curious it may seem, that this people was chosen to be the connecting link for God's unique revelation to the nations, and yet that it has failed and lost its qualification as the chosen people." [45]

To cite a more specific illustration of the meaning in the sheer arrangement of the Bible, in the Hebrew text of the Old Testament, Ezra and Nehemiah are placed prior to Chronicles. Chronicles thus becomes the last book of the Old Testament. In that structure, then, the Old Testament ends with the statement of Cyrus on behalf of the reconstruction of the Temple. The exegetical meaning of that placement is that the Old Testament as a whole is intended to be read as a book that is not yet finished. The story is to be continued. To cite one New Testament illustration of the same kind of strategy, The Acts of the Apostles is regarded by Watanabe as having been placed in its present position intentionally, to serve as the key to the understanding of the Gospels and the epistles. "In the fourth century the church realized this by placing it in its present position in the New Testament. They thereby permanently determined the nature and value of the book." [46]

Finally, the understanding of the Bible as the canon of the church recognizes thereby a unity without which the Bible could often seem an inherently contradictory book.

Several of Watanabe's favorite allusions can be cited. The Song of Solomon, judged by the customary canons of literary criticism, is a pagan love song that leaves a Christian reader unedified. When one asks the question as to why it was included by the church in the canon, however, it becomes clear that this Song was intended to be a hymn of praise to God, whose bride was Israel and is now the church. Again, in the epistle to the Romans it is said that Abraham was justified by faith. In The Epistle of James it is said that the Christian is justified by works. Which is the proper expression of the Christian way? One who interprets the Bible as the canon of the church need not choose between these two positions. As long as it is known that the Bible is the canon of the church, it is understood that nothing is in the Bible fortuitously. Therefore, before an interpreter acts precipitously, he should ask himself what the church must have had in mind in including such materials. When he does so with respect to this particular issue, he can take the message of the two epistles at face value. For the church has understood John 6:28 and 29 as reconciling the apparent contradiction. The meanings of these texts are embraced in the Johannine understanding that the work that justifies is precisely the work in which one believes that Jesus is the Christ. Interpretations that merely state the oppositions in the Bible, therefore, or which make an effort to harmonize them, are wrong. Apparent oppositions are to be read in the light of the canonical intention of the church, which becomes the basis for overcoming opposition by a strategy of reconciliation.[47]

Japanese scholars, who are characteristically reserved about the accomplishments of their own number, have nevertheless spoken of Watanabe as a towering mountain in the range of Japanese theologians. Two things could be meant by this. He has achieved eminence among his colleagues. As they themselves say, his work has a comprehensiveness and unity seldom seen " even in foreign works " on the same theme.[48] On the other hand, he stands alone. No school has developed around his view. A school, however, is not in Watanabe's expectation. He has submitted a method that should challenge and illuminate theological development in Protestant Japan. Most commanding of all, however, is the implication of his view for the Non-Church movement. Since the appearance of Watanabe's work, Non-Church Christians ought not to be able to proceed with equanimity apart from a more serious consideration of the ecclesiological backgrounds of Biblical interpretation. It has become apparent in this study that there is a dualism in their position that has permitted their intellectuals the luxury of detached investigation in the academic study and almost fundamentalistic tactics in the Bible class. The historical method of interpretation prevails in the classrooms, the allegorical and dogmatic methods prevail in the Bible classes. The interpretation of the Bible as the canon of the church, however, is a hermeneutical science that calls for the end of that dualism and suggests a method by which it can be overcome. The price of the method is participation in the church as in some sense the Christian's inalienable home.

II | The Theology of Church Existence

THE DOMINANT THEOLOGY OF JAPAN AND THE FIRST TO ISSUE in a systematic theology is the work of Yoshitaka Kumano, professor at the Tokyo Union Theological Seminary. The one thing all Christendom is most apt to know about Japanese Christianity is the existence of its powerful and creative Non-Church movement. The churches outside Japan should, therefore, be interested to discover the point of view of Japan's most influential Protestant theologian, for he takes the position that the mediation of the church is the essential fact of the Christian religion.

Why this most Westernized of all the leading Japanese theologians should be so influential often seems mystifying. His books are written in a heavy, classical style. His sentences are aphoristic, interfering with the smoothness and symmetry that one comes to associate with systematic thinking. For the content of his works he is heavily reliant upon Western sources, even though he has never studied, lived, or even traveled outside Japan. As a public lecturer and preacher he avails himself of almost no homiletical projection. Most puzzling of all is that his three major works, published between 1933 and the present time, appear to adopt successively different points of departure. One could almost assume they were written by different men.

Patient analysis of the works of Kumano, however, reveals that he has assimilated the finest expressions of Christianity. He has made these insights available to Japanese Christianity as the very ground of its authentic life. That he has made the insights his own can be detected in a subtle continuity in his literature. His first work, *Eschatology and Philosophy of History*,[1] was an effort to distinguish the Christian view of history from faiths and philosophies whose world views often resemble Christianity. Christianity, he proposed, is not a way of looking at the world, characterized in world views by reflection, resignation, intellectualizing, and adaptation to culture. Christianity is rather a way of overcoming the world, through creation, action, and the decisiveness of the will. What faith needs is not a world view but venture and decisiveness that lend dynamic to man's action in the world. One who understands that about Christianity understands the meaning of eschatology. Eschatology has for Kumano the connotation developed for it by Ernst Troeltsch and his pupil Friedrich Gogarten. Eschatology in Kumano's position refers not to the so-called last things but to the foundation of temporal existence.

The end of time and history is at the same time the foundation of events which come about in history and in time. . . . Eschatology is not about the future of temporal existence but about temporal existence itself. The task of eschatology is not to put an end to history but to interpret the eschatological character of temporal, historical existence.[2]

This work has the distinction of being the first book on Christian thought to be applauded and seriously encountered by non-Christian intellectuals in Japan.

Outline of Christianity [3] was Kumano's next major work. "Many lines of this book were written with tears," the author confesses in his preface, for a large part was composed toward the end of the war in the shock of bereavement. The marked characteristic of this volume is the way in which the more radical existential perspectives of his first work give way to ecclesiological perspectives. The existence with which Christianity has to do here is not existence in time so much as the very special form that existence takes in the church. Christianity is a historical and social reality. One must understand it by grasping its eternal reality from within the phenomenal reality. To do so one must start not with ideas about religion but with the concrete existence of religion, with religious reality, which means in the case of Christianity, with the church.[4] Here it seems that the accent in the *Church Dogmatics* of Karl Barth has dominated the historicist and existentialist motifs of Kumano's earlier work. He then seems prepared to proceed to the development of a *Dogmatik* patterned along Barthian lines.

On the surface, the first two volumes of his *Dogmatics* [5] bear this out. In outline and even in format they suggest an abridged version of Barth's momentous work. That fact ought not be regarded as something to deplore. In the context of a form of Christianity that deliberately strives to be Japanese and in a period in Japanese culture when there was some real advantage to be seized by nationally self-conscious efforts, the embracing of so Western a point of view as Barth's ought not be regarded as an act of sheer imitation. For Kumano, however, it is a matter of Christian conviction that theology be developed from within the conditions of the church catholic and not from within the conditions of Japanese culture.

If that is understood, then the continuity in his work begins to manifest itself. His first major work was an effort to dissociate Christianity from religious points of view that emerge out of cultural situations. His second work was an effort to delineate the Christianity that emerges within conditions of existence where Christ is the Lord of life. Only after establishing this dialectic between existence and *ekklēsia* was it considered safe to write a dogmatic theology. Kumano's dogmatics is based on the assumption that Christianity is a historical faith. What is meant by history had already been defined by him. History refers to the contingency of life that becomes evident in man's temporality when death threatens and when God reveals that he is the boundary, the limit, the end of all human possibilities. That definition is the meaning of eschatology which was developed in the first volume. History also refers to the Christian faith, initiated in God's act of self-revelation in Christ, communicated through time by Christ's body, the church, and forming man's existence in the present. That is the meaning of what he calls " Christian phenomenology " in the second volume. The *Dogmatics* is built upon these twin assumptions about history. History in this later work is the eschatological overcoming of the evanescent conditions of human existence through the eternal God's witness to himself in the life of the church. In such a setting, dogmatic theology is the intellectual service of church existence, or what might be called an ecclesiological existentialism. The strength of Kumano's contribution is that although he is strongly Barthian in his recent work, he never wholly forgets what he learned from Troeltsch and Gogarten.

A theology of church existence raises the question, however, as to whether Kumano does not abrogate the possibility of an indigenous Japanese theology. By deliberate strategy his view seeks to go beneath Japanese existence to human existence, and it seeks to transcend Japanese history in the direction of the holy history of the Christian community, a preponderantly Western phenomenon. Admittedly Kumano's intention is less indigenous than the intention of the Non-Church Christians. "If it is possible to create a Japanese theology," he says, "we must seek the basis for such an attempt in the understanding of the historic faith." [6] That must not be taken to mean, however, that he has no sense of destiny as a Japanese theologian. "The Japanese Church," he says, "may be able to contribute to a resolution of the fateful division of the Western church by strengthening the will to establish the evangelical faith and to recover the Bible at points at which Protestantism and Roman Catholicism should agree." [7] Nor should it be overlooked that Kumano was a student of the Presbyterian pastor-theologian Masahisa Uemura, whom he knew long before he knew Barth or Gogarten, and who himself had a passion for encouraging theological independence in Japanese Christians. Kumano attributes to Uemura's counsel the start he got with the problem of eschatology. Moreover, although Kumano's *Dogmatics* has striking resemblances to Barth's *Church Dogmatics*, no other theme was more central to the writings of his teacher Uemura than the doctrine of the church.

In the setting of Japanese theology today, the distinctive elements in Kumano's theology cluster around two emphases. The first is a nonapocalyptic view of eschatology that is the best expression of his existentialism. The second is a dualistic view of church tradition, the best approach to his high ecclesiology. The most helpful way I know to present his theology of church existence is to elaborate these two distinctive elements and then, in conclusion, to illustrate how they combine in the statement of his dogmatics.

I

The subject of eschatology for Kumano is not history but God. It is not even history in respect of its future, its " last " things. Eschatology does not have to do with events occurring after death and the situation surrounding life then. In that sense, Kumano's eschatology is nonapocalyptic. That is, it does not describe some sudden change in the circumstances of the observable world. The apocalyptic statements of Jesus and the disciples are not thereby repudiated. They are only dissociated from eschatology. The event of Jesus and not his sayings and teachings inspires Christian eschatology.[8]

> The world waits for the incarnation of God. Until the perfect dialectical unity of eternity and time realizes itself, time knows neither eternity nor itself. In order to save time, God becomes incarnate. Only in God in history does man know both God and himself. Christianity is based upon God in history. . . . Revelation is a historical event in which history reveals its eschatological character.[9]

This connotation which dominated his earliest work is still prevalent in his later work. As he says there, eschatology does not have to do with the perishing of the world or the dissolving of history but with man standing at the boundary of the world or at the end of history and there seeing God.[10] The Holy Spirit, for instance, is said to be an eschatological reality because it is the Spirit who makes us breathe eternity within this world and gives us the foretaste of eternal life.[11]

As has been indicated earlier, two senses of the word

" history " emerge from this understanding of eschatology. One has to do with the limited conditions of man's existence in time. The other has to do with the overcoming of this limit through God's revelation. Like the English language, the Japanese language has only one word for history, and that word is weighted with connotations that cannot begin to suggest the dynamics to which the word " history " points. The Japanese word is *reki-shi.* It is made up of two syllables that, separately, mean " calendar " and " chronicle." Therefore, to denote the form of history that is man's existence toward death, the German word *Geschichtlichkeit,* or " historicity," is used. To denote the form of history man has when God is at man's end, the expression " true history " is used. Eschatology, which embraces both these meanings of history, becomes a dialectical movement between anthropology and revelation, that is, between existence toward death and existence under God.[12]

Anthropology in Kumano's view is the study of man as a being " who is destined to die as a sinner." [13] It is quite consistent, therefore, that Kumano makes anthropology a branch of eschatology and yet contends that the subject of eschatology is God. For anthropology elaborates a circular situation that eventually turns the study of man into theology. The circle can be stated in this way: " Man knows God only when he faces death "; [14] yet, " man grasps the meaning of life and death only through God." [15] What is the significance of this circle? When man lives through time, he experiences the acts comprising his time as finite and perishable acts. Man's time prophesies his death. Man yearns for eternity, but only God is eternal. When man's temporal existence is placed under the higher light of God's eternity, he experiences his temporality as guilt. Guilt in this sense is not a moral term, of course, but a deeply historical, that is, a personal term indicating the meaninglessness of a life that ends in death.

"God and death are completely different, but both threaten our existence in the same way."[16] God is the being who *forms* man's existence. Death is the abyss that *terminates* man's existence. God and death, therefore, both point to the same truth about man: he is perishable. But death and God are both experienced by the temporal man as an abyss of fear. The true character of death, however, is only understood in the presence of God. Until then the fear of God and the fear of death are confused, and that confusion Kumano calls "sin." Presumably Kumano means that not to know that it is God who is at one's end is to live in sin.[17]

What does man fear in death? Not the end of life. No Japanese theologian could assert that convincingly, considering the long and noble history of suicide in Japan. What he fears in death is "the task of immortality." How can the impure soul be immortal? The ethically sensitive, says Kumano, are terrified by that question.[18] For an ethically sensitive attitude toward immortality would elicit a feeling of condemnation, considering the implicit individualism of immortality. In death a man cannot think simply of his isolated pilgrimage in an afterlife. He has a responsibility to the others from whom death would cut him off. The death of one person hurts another person. Death destroys the love relation. "I betray thy love in my death and thy death destroys my hope."[19] Death is a problem to man, not in his privacy then, but in his community with others. "Death cancels all our personal pronouns."[20] That is why Christianity, basing itself as it does on the loving relation of persons, regards suicide as sin. It is an escape from responsibility. Death ends the possibility for assuming responsibility for others. Therefore, it introduces the fear more basic than the fear of death. That fear, about which the Biblical faith is concerned, is the fear of Ultimate Judgment, which the Christian faith interprets as estrangement from God.

The solution to the fears man's " historicity " evokes is given in the " true history " of the Christian revelation. The judgment of history is seen where faith is based on the event of eternity becoming time. The word become flesh is itself the ultimate judgment of history. Faith is the attitude of waiting for light even though in a world of darkness. Faith is dependence upon a world in which there is no sorrow, tears, or death, in which the Almighty God alone is the ruler, and in which man is stripped of all vanity. There man knows the meaning of history for the first time.[21]

This understanding of history is structured largely by Gogarten's social understanding of revelation. History is the place where an I and a Thou meet. The I exists where the Thou exists. It is not simply that the I exists first and then comprehends the existence of others. Rather, the Thou is the reality that calls out the I. It is in that call that the I is first called I. In the presence of the call, one must choose to accept or to reject. The decision is what is known as history.

The true history, however, is the history in which God's act in Christ's resurrection from the dead overcomes our dying life. True history for man is the history of God's grace. When man does not accept the call of God's grace, he has no history in the true sense. That is why the gospel is called eschatological. It overcomes man's illusions about history and creates a new, true history.

History in this connotation concerns only man. The end to which this *eschaton* refers is not some change in the circumstances of the world, objectively understood. The fact of death, for instance, is an objective fact. But the death of a single person is not an objective fact. It is subjective, that is, a fact of a man's personal existence, of his history. The end of the world is in the same sense a subjective (*shutai*) reality.[22] "We do not know the conditions of existence beyond death. But we are not disappointed by this lack. Our eschatology, therefore, is different from the daydreaming stories of the heathen." [23]

As in dialectical theology, Kumano supplants the traditional distinction between nature and the supernatural by the distinction between time and eternity. In this he is also instructed by the work of his fellow countryman, Seiichi Hatano. The effect of this position is to throw the accent upon life in history rather than upon life beyond history. To say that in Christ the Word became flesh means that eternity has taken over the responsibility for time. This for Kumano is the gospel. The gospel sets time within God's plan, thus saving time from fallenness. That is what it means to say the election of Christ was before the foundation of the world: it is an eternal decision about time. It is also why the Scriptures " always " refer to the pre-existence and the return of Christ in the same breath. Both pre-existence and return refer to the good news about eternity's redemption of time.[24] Thus it is also understandable why the subject of eschatology, as Kumano uses it, manages to bypass the problem of describing the conditions of life after death. For eschatology is a reality most meaningfully related to everyday life.[25]

When Kumano says that Christianity is a historical religion, he does not mean simply that Christianity has a rich experience that comes from a long historical existence. He means Christianity has to do with an event of personal revelation that creates history.[26] The true historical faith is the body of an eternal mediator that has become a constant formative force in man's existence. As such, it ought not to be referred to as the history of a faith, for it is a faith that is itself history.[27] The power of Christ to form the history that constitutes man's very life is what is meant by eschatology. Revelation has an eschatological character in the sense that it puts the world in a completely new and different situation.[28]

II

How does the eschatological faith express itself through the mediation of history? This ultimately is a question of the relation between the incarnate Christ and the historical church. The true historical faith is the body of the eternal mediator constantly becoming a formative force in Christian existence. But what, indeed, is the eternal mediator? Is it Jesus Christ, the Bible, the church, or the creeds and dogmas of the church? Kumano's answer is that ecclesiology is an extension of Christology, but that Christology is therefore never quite completed. Christology is completed only as the Word of God in Christ, conserved by the church in its history, is renewed in present history, forming the life of the church.[29]

Church existence, which is formed by the eschatological event of God's incarnation in Jesus Christ, takes the form primarily of tradition. Church tradition in Kumano's work, however, is a dualistic notion. Interestingly for his purpose, the Japanese language has two words for tradition. One is *dentō*, which pertains to tradition in its historical pastness. The other is *denshō*, which is tradition as a living witness, creating the conditions for the future. Revelation produces tradition as witness, but that tradition is not revelation. Tradition as witness becomes conserved in tradition as past history, and that tradition is faith in one legitimate and significant mode of its being. Tradition as past history always retains the formative power of witness. Tradition as witness in turn expresses itself as the historical church that becomes past. Faith in the revelation, therefore, is not in contradiction with tradition as past history (*dentō*). The true tradition as history is not simply life in memory of the past. It rather gives rise to tradition as witness that compels decision for the future, forming the church's life.[30]

In evangelical theology, tradition as past history (*dentō*) has the character of catholicity. "Our theology is catholic," Kumano confesses. "The Christian exists within the existence of the church. No matter how confessional or individualistic your theology is, it should aim to be catholic. . . . The infinite freedom of theology comes from its willingness to be bound in the service of the church. Theology is a function of the church."[31] Hence Kumano can assent to the Roman Catholic doctrine that "outside the church there is no salvation." Church existence is the necessary presupposition for faith.[32]

Tradition as witness (*denshō*) is the faith of the church expressing itself in eschatological power, forming the church out of the world. When tradition as witness arises in response to the free grace of God and the existence of the believer is formed by this act of confession, tradition cannot be viewed as something closed. It is always open. Kumano believes that this openness in the evangelical view of tradition distinguishes his so-called catholic view of tradition from the *Roman* Catholic view. "We respect tradition as witness as well as tradition as history," he says, "and thirst for the gifts of the free spirit."[33]

Tradition as past history is twenty centuries of the fleshly embodiment of apostolic tradition as witness. The church must convert its historical tradition into living witness in every age or else tradition will harden into voiceless forms of flesh. That again is the danger of the Roman Catholic tradition, which allows the sacramental tradition to supplant or at least to supersede the tradition of the Word. If tradition existed only at the level of *dentō*, the continuity of the church through history would be intrinsic, immanental, or natural. Where the tradition is, there would the church be. A sacramental tradition is of that sort. Considering the dualism of tradition, however, the church has its continuity not in its conservation of the past tradition but in its witness. Where the church defaults in witness, it ceases to exist as church.

The other side of the problem is equally serious. If tradition were only witness, without past history, the Church would dwindle off into irresponsible subjectivity (*shukansei*). The two forms of tradition should be held together without confusion and without separation, like the two natures of Christ in the Chalcedonian formula. Another analogy less frequently used but somewhat more suggestive is taken from the relation between justification and sanctification. The two traditions must not be identified. Growth would thereby be discouraged, just as growth in the Christian life would be discouraged if justification exhausted all the possibilities of sanctification. Nor should the two be separated. Such a separation would suggest that sanctification constitutes a revision of justification, or that living witness (*denshō*) is at liberty to alter past history (*dentō*).

The Non-Church attitude is believed by Kumano to be based upon the separation of justification and sanctification. The Non-Church group takes the position that the church is sinful, and that therefore Christianity must enter a new and separate phase called Non-Church. The only strategy they have of purifying tradition is to separate from it.[34] Kumano, on the other hand, believes that the evangelical faith, in the way it holds the dualism of tradition in unity, prevents Christianity from becoming either a dead orthodoxy or an uncontrollable subjectivism.[35]

However much this discussion may seem prejudiced on the side of tradition as living witness, it is tradition as past history that provides the subject matter for theology. It is the task of theology to study the creeds of the ancient catholic period, especially the ecumenical creeds, which are largely Trinitarian and Christological in character.[36] The creeds of the church are considered the best expression of the unique activity of the church. "The church is where the word is rightly declared and the Sacraments rightly administered," as the Augsburg confession affirms. But that definition of the church describes only its activity, neglecting its existential ground. In the history of the church there have been three conditions for the existence of the church: canon, creed, and ministry. The canon of the Bible is fixed. The ministry varies in form as the church's life develops. The creeds stand between the canon, which is fixed, and the ministry, which is variable, and thus provide the best expression of the church's proper activity.[37]

The original creeds were the confessions of faith of new converts. These creeds eventually opened themselves to two possible attitudes. They could be treated as rules of faith whose dogmatic content was beyond rationality. Or they could be treated as grateful responses to an act of grace. The reformers desired to conserve the original sense of the creed, and it is the deliberate intention of Kumano, notwithstanding the critical attitude of the Non-Church group in his country, to call the modern church to a revival of interest in the creeds, although in a Protestant and evangelical spirit. This involves, not blind adherence to written documents as Non-Church devotees fear, but an investigation of the meaning of the creed by going behind it to the Biblical tradition that originally inspired it. The creeds and confessions of the church that began as praise and repentance must become the practical action of reasonable men transmuted into an intellectual operation. That, according to Kumano, is the essential feature of an evangelical theology.[38]

How can a theology that is so deliberately dependent upon the existence of the church avoid endorsing denominationalism? According to Kumano, it is impossible for theology to be undenominational. Tradition as history (*dentō*) includes the fact of the plurality of churches. To say that if theology were based on the Bible, there would be only one theology and one church is a most abstract way of thinking. The way to save theology from being denominational is precisely to know how one's denomination has originated from within the Catholic tradition. Rather than calling upon the denominations to dissolve themselves, Kumano is urging them to go behind their traditions as history (*dentō*) in order to recover the tradition as witness (*denshō*) that originally gave rise to their churches.[39]

The Bible is part of the tradition as witness. That is the truth in the Non-Church movement's preoccupation with the Bible. As witness, however, the Bible has created the church. Hence, evangelical Protestants, very much as Roman Catholics, interpret the Bible from the standpoint of their existence within the church that the Bible has formed. That is the truth of Watanabe's theory of the interpretation of the Bible *as* the canon of the church. The difference between Kumano and Roman Catholicism on the inspiration of the Bible is more pronounced, however, than the difference between Watanabe and Roman Catholicism. In Roman Catholicism the theory of Biblical inspiration derives from the fact of the canonization of the Bible. The Bible is authoritative because the inspired church canonized it. Up to this point Roman Catholicism and Watanabe very nearly agree. They simply draw different inferences. In Roman Catholicism the fact that the church confers authority on the Bible gives church tradition priority over the Bible. In Watanabe, the church is only the instrument of canonization. The Bible in its self-assertion remains over against the church as its norm and critic.

Kumano, however, believes that " the Bible itself made the church decide that the Bible is the canon." [40] The Bible was inspired before it was canonized. It is the subject of the tradition it forms, and for that reason stands over against the tradition as its judge. The church knows the Bible is inspired when it becomes aware that its own obedience is inspired by God's free grace as mediated in the Bible. " The absolute authority of the Bible is in giving the knowledge of God and the certainty of salvation. I found the way of the church-forming tradition in this authority," he has said.[41]

Like Watanabe, Kumano believes that the special nature of the Bible requires a special method of interpreting the Bible. It is not adequate to read it by the methods one uses on other forms of literature. Not that those methods are disallowed. It is only that they do not yield what the Bible purports to give. Kumano believes Luther made this clear in his reformation of the Roman tradition. For Luther the purport of the Bible is the knowledge of God revealed in Jesus Christ. When one reads the Bible he should hear the commands and promises of God in Christ. If his methods of reading do not bring him to that result, he should revise his methods. The consequence for Luther was to abandon the traditional allegorical method of interpretation and to stress what he called the strict meaning of the text.[42]

Unlike Watanabe, Kumano's theory of Biblical interpretation encourages what Kumano calls " scientific freedom " with the text. When Watanabe sponsors the reformation view of the " self-interpretation " of the text, he places the emphasis on staying with the whole text until apparent contradictions are overcome. Kumano opens the door to purging the text in the light of the text. That is why he can show some sympathy for Rudolf Bultmann's existential hermeneutic and its project of demythologizing. According to Kumano, demythologizing aims to clarify how the eternal Word wears theological symbols.[43] One cannot come to a right understanding of the revelation by blind obedience to the symbols, which is the mistake of fundamentalism, or by a rationalistic explaining away of the myth, which was the mistake of much of modern theology. Demythologizing is a dehistoricizing of tradition as past in order to rehistoricize through tradition as witness. That is, the tradition as past history (*dentō*) must be interpreted to allow its witness (*denshō*) to appear, forming the existence of the church. Bultmann means almost precisely the same by " demythologizing." Earlier, Kumano had said that the faith must be eschatologized. He repeats that emphasis in his *Dogmatics*, indicating that he prefers the term " eschatologizing " to the term " demythologizing," although the terms mean the same to him. " Exegesis is the eschatological activity of man. The situation that arises from the subjective (*shutaiteki*) act of obedience to the word of God requires immediate interpretation." [44] In Kumano's view, the situation created by obedience to the word of God is the existence of the church. The systematic interpretation of that existence is what is meant by dogmatics.

III

One of the most convincing signs of the maturity of a Christian people is the emergence among them of a dogmatic theology. The reason is that a dogmatic theology assumes the responsibility for stating the totality of the Christian faith in such a way as to manifest the interior coherence of the faith. Successful fulfillment of that responsibility requires intimate and disciplined participation in the faith itself, which usually comes in the wake of a long and committed history of faith.

Some feel that a shadow could be thrown over Kumano's *Dogmatics* if one were to notice its heavy reliance upon the work of Karl Barth. That scarcely seems fair in the light of the fact that theologians in other parts of the world, such as Otto Weber of Göttingen, Hermann Diem of Tübingen, and T. F. Torrance of Edinburgh rely even more heavily on Barth, yet without jeopardy to their professional usefulness. President Hidenobu Kuwada, in reviewing the second volume of Kumano's *Dogmatics*, has not only observed this dependence; he has indicated the irony of it, coming as it does at the precise moment when the Japanese people are losing interest in Karl Barth.[45] Yet, as Kuwada long ago pointed out about Kumano, although he depends heavily on Western sources, he always adds something significant of his own.[46]

Kumano's sympathy in his *Dogmatics* is consistently with Barth. His dependence, however, is only superficially obvious. The form of the *Dogmatics,* for instance, seems identical to Barth's. After his prolegomenon, he moves as Barth does to the doctrine of God. God is Trinity, and the meaning of the Trinity is predestination, which is God's eternal will to save and his perfect creation through the agency of his Son. The Trinitarian doctrine of God then provides the outline for Kumano's dogmatics in the same way it does for Barth. Creation is informed by the theology of the Father; salvation, by the theology of the Son; and sanctification, by the theology of the Holy Spirit. An even more conspicuous similarity is Kumano's adoption of Barth's view of predestination, which is a radical revision of the orthodox concept of predestination. This revision will be discussed more in detail further on.

The differences between Kumano and Barth, however, are equally conspicuous. For one thing, Kumano has chosen to do what Barth refused to do, namely, to concentrate his ethics in one volume, separable from the *Dogmatics*. Hence, Kumano's ethics is being written in the interim between Vols. II and III of his *Dogmatics*. Barth, on the other hand, has kept his ethics inseparably tied to his dogmatics, primarily as a witness that Christian ethics is necessarily theological ethics. In 1954 and 1955, the Japanese violated Barth's intention by isolating the ethics sections of his *Church Dogmatics* into a four-volume translation called *Christian Ethics* (*Kirisutokyō Rinri*). It is hard to believe this project had Barth's approval, considering the fact that since 1928 he has had his complete ethics in manuscript form and has resisted all seduction by publishers. Kumano's rationale for his own separation of ethics from the context of dogmatics, however, is entirely pragmatic. He believes that the Japanese Church needs an understanding of Christian ethics that is best served by treating the subject accessibly, in a monograph.

The doctrine of the Trinity in Kumano, to cite another distinction from Barth, is discussed under the heading of the doctrine of God rather than in the prolegomenon, as Barth does it. The dualistic view of tradition takes the place of the Trinity in Kumano's prolegomenon, setting the method for dogmatics in which church existence is more deliberately at the center than Trinitarian theology is. This decision does not diminish Kumano's Trinitarian loyalties, of course, because the existence of the church is mainly characterized by its creedal history, and its creeds are mainly affirmations of a Trinitarian and Christological sort. The importance of the decision is simply in its insistence upon concrete conditions for the elaboration of the Christian faith that life in the historical church provides. It could be conjectured that Kazoh Kitamori's critique of Barth's Trinitarian prolegomenon as an abstract method has deterred Kumano from following Barth at this point.[47] It may be more plausible, however, to concede that the emphasis on ecclesiological existentialism was already prepared for, as I have indicated, in Kumano's own theological literature.

A theology that makes church existence its point of departure is an effort to avoid the abstractness of metaphysics without falling into the relativity of anthropology. Metaphysical theology is concerned with a transcendental realm beyond the world of experience, whereas Kumano believes that the theological reason should be concerned with our experience in the church. What he means by church experience, however, ought not to be confused with the theologies of the nineteenth century that understood the faith in terms of man's *experience* of faith. A theology of church existence is written, not out of the experience that Christians have in the church, but out of the tradition of the church that conserves the eschatological faith, a faith that stands over against our experience and makes it possible.

Inasmuch as only two of the projected four or five volumes of Kumano's *Dogmatics* have been printed at this writing, it is impossible to anticipate the conclusions of the full outline of his position. Therefore, I will simply illustrate from a few pivotal doctrines how his theology of church existence is already beginning to illuminate certain emphases in the Christian faith.

1. *Predestination.* As in Karl Barth, the doctrine of predestination is the sum and substance of the gospel for Kumano. Predestination is an eschatological doctrine that is communicated in the tradition of the chosen community, the church. The difference between this view and the view of classical Calvinism is patent when it is known that for Kumano as for Barth the object of predestination is one man only, Jesus Christ. " In Jesus Christ God's election has been fulfilled." All other election is based on him.[48] Predestination in this sense means that through Jesus Christ, who is the eternal Word of God under conditions of human history, God chooses man for salvation. In Jesus Christ, God manifests his desire for fellowship with man. That this expression is to be understood as a free act of God in his overflowing mercy is the meaning of predestination.[49]

The doctrine of predestination is called an eschatological doctrine because the predestinating act is not known through world history. It is known only through the revelation of the being, the act, and the promise of God in Jesus Christ. " This *eschaton* evokes the eschatological involvement of the world." Even though the event is in world history, it fundamentally alters our consciousness of history. The eternal word of God's election of man to salvation cuts through the relativities of history as an eternal event, an *eschaton.*[50]

2. *Creation.* The foundation of the doctrine of Creation is not to be found in the natural world but in the historical world. The doctrine of a created world is an eschatological doctrine that has emerged in the history of faith. The meaning of the doctrine is that the world is ruled eternally by God. The Creation stories, therefore, are not simply remnants of mythology. They express a historical consciousness. They are a theology, a form of Biblical proclamation

that states that the creative act of God is essentially one with eschatology. That is, creation depends upon God's free act. The history of Israel is the archetype of the gracious act of God for the whole world. The entire world owes its reality to God. It is called forth by God's formative power. *Creatio ex nihilo* is another way of saying that creation is God's free act. It has nothing to do with ontology or even with the science of the genesis of the world. It simply affirms that the world, like God's people, finds its meaning in God.[51]

Thus, while elevating the doctrine of Creation in this way may give encouragement to science,[52] more significantly it saves the Christian from the necessity for apologizing to natural science for its view of creation.[53] Creation and natural science do not point to the same reality. Creation is a concept primarily historical and not primarily natural. That is not to say, however, that a doctrine of Creation can bypass what scientists deal with as nature. "The history of the world is constituted on the ground of nature. Therefore, God accompanies the preservation of history with the preservation of nature. That is, the Lord of history is almost immediately confessed as the Lord of nature." [54] Volume II of his *Dogmatics* continually asserts Kumano's displeasure with what he regards as Bultmann's excessive neglect of nature categories. In that, Kumano is at one with a majority of Western scholars. However, he at least has the distinction of knowing that the doctrine of Creation is not the church's point of contact with natural science and that the Biblical faith is primarily involved with historical categories, that is, with questions about the final meaning of existence. I believe it could be shown that in this understanding he is more consistent and rigorous than his alleged Continental prototype, Karl Barth.

3. *Anthropology*. One must exercise considerable caution in dealing with the theology of man. The Bible gives no primary place to it, and in the history of the faith theological concerns have always been prior to anthropological concerns – until the nineteenth century. Modern theology made human confrontations methodologically prior to the confrontation with God. The Bible, however, makes God's eternal election of man to salvation the primary datum.

Christian anthropology cannot ignore the *experience* of the Christian, however. That experience can be theologically authentic and protected against the anthropological excesses of nineteenth-century theology if it is regarded as the historical experience of the church itself, and not just the experience of the private Christian. The contents of a theological anthropology are derivable from the existence of believers where that existence is concretely located within the church, understood as the place where the eternal God is creating the new man by his grace. The church can thus become the source of the Christian understanding of man for two inseparable reasons. In the first place, no man can understand himself apart from an encounter with another. The church provides for that encounter, not simply because it is a fellowship of Christians, but because it is the place where Jesus Christ, the true man, is met. Jesus Christ is the neighbor in relation to whom a man may know himself concretely and individually. The relation is not accidental, because it is the purpose of Christ to urge himself upon us as the basis for our meaningful life. In the second place, it is in the church that we encounter the classical creeds whose intention it is to express the mode of existence of the man Jesus. His way of life becomes the basis for our self-understanding through the mediation of the church tradition.

What does an individual find out about himself within the Christ relation that the church provides? He discovers that he is a " new man " whose image of God is rehabilitated as the spiritual possibility for living in community. Man is not a spirit by nature. Yet a spiritual nature is his only possibility of living in the kind of community Christians know as the church. The image of God in man is the possibility of that spiritual communion, but sin is what blocks a man's realization of his manhood and hinders his role in community formation.[55] The knowledge given in Christ involves the two main poles of anthropology. First, sin is revealed as the burden of the entire human race. It has come about by the loss of the fundamental freedom of man to live as a spirit in communion with others. This task of anthropology is to describe man's historical sin by way of the secret of the personality of Jesus.[56] Second, Jesus Christ relieves the burden of sin by restoring man's freedom toward God and thus the possibility of community with the fellow man. " This fact is the foundation for every Christian life: that God is God and man is man, and that this truth is grasped only through the real freedom which Christ as the revealer of the essential man communicates." [57]

4. *The Church.* The essence of the Catholic Church is *communio sanctorum* and *corpus Christi*. The church is an eschatological reality in human history, because it is the historical realization of eternal life.[58] Eternal life is not simply immortality but " the perfected mode of the communion of saints." [59] The very possibility of history is community, and history is nothing but the history of communities.[60] The world, however, is genuinely historical for the first time only as it reflects the body of Christ. One might even say that world history is nothing but the history of the Church Catholic. That claim represents the historical consciousness

of the Christian faith.[61] The doctrine of providence, therefore, is understandably supportive of the doctrine of the church, referring as it does to the unchangeability of Christ and hence to the preservation of the church in the midst of this world's confusion. For the sake of the church, "God preserves everything else by providence."[62]

5. *Ethics*. Christian ethics is an ethics of personal and communal responsibility. An ethical act is an act that provides history with evidence of a thoroughgoing continuity running through history despite the transience of time. The task of ethics is to raise the question of the possibility of this kind of permanently relevant act. The answer to that question is given in God's gracious act in Christ. In Christ, God has elected us, and that election reveals the eschatological character of being. When God's highest command forms our everyday life, the historical world takes on eschatological reality. Concretely, this means that man's response to God's act in Christ is not exhausted by particular moral actions. God's election in Christ demands the obedience of our total personal existence.[63]

This view of ethics may strike the ear of the Western man, oriented as he is to morality and pragmatism, as being very odd indeed. Actually, Kumano was prepared for it by the dialectical theology to which one of his early works was devoted.[64] Dialectical theology took the position that the unique thing about Christian ethics was not its utilitarian formulations but the power it provided to support these requirements. The prior questions in Christian ethics have to do, not with specific ethical requirements, but with the human existence itself, its life toward death and the tragic character of life in which goodness seems to have no ultimate hope. Thus the root ethical question is, How does the eternal confront my life in the present? One does not ask,

What ought we do? before receiving an answer to What are we? That is to say, in Christian ethics, the indicative precedes the imperative.

This kind of thinking moves against the sort of utilitarianism that characterized much of nineteenth-century theological ethics, just as the ethics of the early church moved against Stoic and Epicurean ethics. It also provides a refreshing contrast with the major non-Christian religion of Japan, which is Buddhism. As Christians, the Japanese are not interested in escaping from this world into the next world, not even into " the pure land " of the next world, to which Buddhism invites them. Rather, they are concerned with how to purify their own land of " defilement and desolation." The Christian's eschatological hope, which involves man in community with God's ultimate purposes in Christ, supports life *in this world* with meaning and gives a reason for realistic action. The action in the world is not the ethic. The ethic is primarily the eschatological dimension of community with God in Christ through the church, which supports our action in the world with ultimate meaning.[65]

So brief a survey is bound to misrepresent Kumano's vast and rich theological position. In one sense, it misrepresents him because he nowhere states his position with such tightness and concision. In another sense, related to this, it misrepresents him because it probably exaggerates the systematic unity of his position, a unity that is surely there but not as obviously there as I have made it seem. Kumano once said, " Faith is a miracle, but theology is not." [66] What he meant was that theology uses the ordinary methods of knowledge by which to elucidate the revelation of God received by the church in Jesus Christ. I would claim that it is little short of a miracle that so distinguished a theology as

Kumano's has appeared within the short span of Christian experience that history records for Japan. Kumano has also observed that when Paul cried out, " O the depth! " he was not sighing. He was praising God.[67] In that context, I can only hope that my somewhat labored attempt to present Kumano's exacting insights has not obscured their doxological lift.

III | *The Theology of the Pain of God*

The theology of Kazoh Kitamori is the most self-consciously Japanese of the current theological tendencies in Japan. Yet it seems the most likely to interest and appeal to the theologians of the West, especially to Americans. For one thing, technical theological concerns are subordinated to the concern for communication. Kitamori is a sensitive stylist who could succeed in Japan as a poet, novelist, or essayist were he not a theologian. As a theologian he addresses the insights of the faith to a broad range of cultural issues from Marxism to *haiku* (a refined form of traditional Japanese poetry). The more academic Christians of Japan tend to dismiss him as one who draws lessons from Christianity for practical living. The truth is, he understands that the theological enterprise must be conducted from within the concrete conditions of human existence. By communication of the faith, therefore, he does not mean simply expressing the faith in easily comprehensible or moving language. He means rethinking the faith and reformulating it in the dimension in which the faith speaks to the fundamental human predicament.

The fundamental human predicament is not a racial or

national characteristic, as Kitamori knows. However, one never exists in abstraction from his tradition. Hence Kitamori refers to Buddhism as " our tradition " in much the same way Paul the apostle identifies himself as a Jew. Penetrating Japanese word studies occur in his writings with the same frequency and illumination with which Martin Heidegger employs studies of old Germanic words. The very fact that nations are located in space means they must seek God from within their locale (Acts 17:26-27). The consequence for Kitamori is that he has written his theology of the pain of God in the same spirit in which he believes the Second Isaiah was written, and with the same justification, " to console and encourage a determined people." [1]

Paramount in his thought, therefore, is involvement in what is apparently as central to the Japanese experience as any other single reality, the experience of suffering. Suffering is the common term that links God, the Christian faith, and Japanese existence. Kitamori is fundamentally convinced that a suffering people such as the Japanese may play a unique role in the holy history of Christianity, as the German spirit did in the sixteenth century, recapturing for the faith of the future a reality in the Biblical faith that is losing ground in the church. The reality to which he refers is the sense of the pain of God, poignantly revealed in Japanese suffering.[2]

The category of pain is grasped by Kitamori with the severest hermeneutical simplicity. Everything he touches is forced to address itself to that interest. Pain is the theologian's stone that interprets all the theological materials. The Japanese call Kitamori's theology a *furoshiki* theology. The *furoshiki* is a square of cloth in which Japanese housewives wrap their groceries, students their books, tradesmen their tools. The metaphor originally had a technical, Hegelian connotation. All antinomies in thought and in life were *aufgehoben*, synthetized, " wrapped up " by Hegel. Kitamori learned this method of dialectical synthesis from his philosophy professor at the University of Kyoto, Hajime Tanabe, a Hegelian philosopher with a Buddhist background. Thus, for instance, in his book *Theology Today* [3] the dialectical opposites in the contemporary theological situation are vigorously attacked by Kitamori. Nothing is wholly lost for a *furoshiki* theology, however. The apparent antagonisms between modern liberalism and Barthianism are finally " wrapped up," therefore, in his own theology of the pain of God.

For Westerners who have been through the Neo-Hegelianism of the late British idealists the Hegelian *furoshiki* is the least convincing and most banal element in Kitamori's work. It closely borders, however, on the most impressive thing about his theology, that is, the unity in his theological interpretation. Every major doctrinal consideration in the customary theological agenda is forced to undergo reformulation in the light of his conclusion concerning the centrality of the pain of God in the Christian faith. At times one gets the impression he carries his principle to extremes. One might even wish to turn against Kitamori the criticism he applies to Marxism. When Marxism makes its position the solution to all problems, he has said, it makes the mistake of overstatement, and overstatement is most unscientific and dogmatic.[4]

I for one prefer to think that Kitamori has a highly acceptable and desirable method that, like Karl Marx's, ought not be judged by its results alone. Like the *furoshiki*, it wraps up everything of importance. Unlike the *furoshiki*, which usually contains items as miscellaneous and disconnected as those found in a Western woman's purse, everything within Kitamori's theological purview clings together inwardly through a single principle of interpretation. He is a systematic theologian in the best sense, where system does not mean a logical structure or an architectonic lamination of related ideas but a living organism that survives in every part by virtue of its throbbing heart.

I

The theology of the pain of God moves on one axis but between two poles. The first pole is indicated in the assertion that "pain is the essence of God."[5] The factor that makes this claim most appealing to the Japanese people makes it least appealing to traditional theology. Traditionally, God is believed to be impassible. That is, suffering is thought to be foreign to his nature.[6] Those who believe the suffering of Jesus Christ is essentially the suffering of God are known as Patripassians, and Patripassianism has been a heresy in the history of the church. Historically a suffering people, the Japanese have been more aware of the compassion of God in Kitamori's view than of the technical theological risks. Unfortunately, however, popular enthusiasm for "the pain of God" is based upon a misapprehension. The pain that God has is not the pain of sympathy or of empathy with man's misfortunes. It is a pain in God's very being as God, connected not so much with man's physical misfortunes as with his sinful estrangement from God.

The second pole in Kitamori's theology is the conviction that "human pain is the expression of God's wrath."[7] This claim is most offensive to the human spirit and least likely to be mentioned by Kitamori's sympathizers. The embarrassment and taciturnity, however, is based upon a misunderstanding. For pain is not *inflicted* upon man by a wrathful God. Existing pain is simply *used* by God as a symbol of his own pain.

These two poles, misunderstood as they are, nevertheless remain the key to Kitamori's point of view. Some care must now be taken to elucidate their meaning in relation to Kitamori's own intention.

The dominant theological influence upon Kitamori has been Lutheran. He is a first-generation Christian who had his theological training in a Lutheran seminary, having experienced his conversion through the ministry of the Lutheran Church. He had read a thesis on Luther by Shigehiko Satō, then professor at the Lutheran Theological Seminary at Tokyo. Moved to a fuller study of Luther, he enrolled in the seminary strictly for that purpose. There he read the Bible over and over and came to know the meaning of grace for himself. He has remained in the *Kyōdan,* however, even though the Lutheran Church made itself independent of the United Church of Japan following the war.

It is no mystery, therefore, that his thinking is a *theologia crucis.* " All theological thinking is deduced from the cross, as it was in Paul," he writes.[8] Today, however, a simple *theologia crucis* is no longer adequate as a theological axiom. Recent theology is to blame for that. On one side, modern liberalism reduced the cross to a simple illustration of God's concern for man. Kitamori calls this view of the cross " love monism," for it does not involve God himself in a moment of pain. On the other side, Karl Barth has sponsored a Trinitarian view of the love of God that makes God's love a reality prior to and apart from man. It is a love that transpires between Father, Son, and Holy Spirit. According to Kitamori, Barth neglects something very important that Luther and Paul saw in the love of God, namely, the pain caused by God's care for the sinner.[9] It is not that Barth does not see what Luther and Paul saw. It is simply that he has not put it at the center of his system. That is, the cross does not have methodological primacy for his theology. In contrast to these recent attitudes toward the cross, Kitamori has put the cross at the methodological center of his system but has guaranteed the precise content of the cross by specifying it as " the pain of God."

What does it mean, then, to say that pain is the very essence of God? It means that God, who loves the unlovable, does so at the price of letting his Son die. The event of the cross is not an event outside the action of God. Indeed, the death of Christ, Kitamori fondly quotes Masahisa Uemura as saying, is in some sense also the death of God. Or as Peter T. Forsyth is frequently quoted as saying, the cross is in the heart of God. It may be surprising to hear that God dies. But if the church ever loses that surprise, *it* is dead.[10] For the church lives by the good news that God is Savior. His role as Savior involves him in pain, the pain of letting his Son die. The news of that pain heals the brokenness of man. Paradoxically, the news of the pain of God is the good news.

What it means that the Son dies can only be interpreted in the context of the wrath of God. God is necessarily against those who betray his love. God the Father therefore faces sinners as a wrathful God. If God were to love a sinner, he would in some sense go out of himself as God. That is, God's relation to the sinner involves God either in the death of the sinner or in a death of his own.[11] The gospel is the announcement that God has chosen to love the sinner, and that therefore he has in some sense gone out of himself; he has in some sense died as God. Kitamori takes this to be the meaning of Phil., ch. 2, in which Paul interprets the event of Christ as God's self-emptying. In that event, God embraces the object of his wrath, which is the sinner, by conquering his wrath. That is his pain. Pain is a third thing in God between love and wrath. It is a synthesis of love and wrath in which the love conquers the wrath. It is not man's sin but God's wrath that accounts for the pain of God. For the pain is the act of swallowing up his wrath.[12]

Three orders of love must, therefore, be seen in the life of God. The first is the love that exists prior to the pain. Here God's love is immediate, as before the Fall of man, where the object of his love is worthy of love. This love is natural and smooth, that is, unhindered. It enjoys the same intensity as exists in natural relations, such as love within a family. When this smooth love is betrayed, however, it turns to wrath. "A betrayed love which does not become wrath is not real love. A God who does not know how to be angry is not God." (Cf. Ezek. 5:13.) [13] The sin of man has produced the effect of wrath in the love of God. Henceforth, only Christ, who is without sin, remains the object of this first order of love.

The second order of love is love that is challenged by pain. Here God reconciles those toward whom he should be angry, and in the process ceases in a sense to be God: that is the essence of the forgiveness of sins. Pain is not simply suffering. It is unrelieved, unresolved suffering. It is the teeth in suffering.[14] The pain is God in conflict with himself, God going outside of himself in Christ, God letting his Son die: all of which means God conquering his wrath by his love in the interests of loving the unloveworthy.

The third order of love is love that is based on the pain of God. This is the love that forgives the sinner through pain and in the act overcomes the sinner and creates the conditions for obedience to God. Here something of the smoothness of the first order of love is regained. This is the order of redemption and of sanctification, therefore the order that is only eschatologically realizable. Wherever this order of love appears in this world it appears in brokenness.

We hold it only in hope. Therefore, in Kitamori's theology it is the second order that is the theological axiom, the order of love challenged by pain.[15]

Kitamori's sense of the neglect of this axiom in modern theology led him to write a book with the rather misleading title, *Theology Today*. Japanese theological students turn to this little book for a survey of major concerns in present-day theology only to find everything " wrapped up " in Kitamori's theological *furoshiki*. Every theological view from Schleiermacher to the present is tested for its attitude toward *Schmerz* in God. Where no *Schmerz* is found, the theology is found wanting. It cannot be denied, however, that Kitamori makes his case against modern theology stick. Modern theology is principally deficient because it has no place for a conflict between wrath and love in God; therefore it does not understand the pain of God, and by that same token the cross remains an instrument of suffering without teeth. Ritschl rightly characterized Schleiermacher's theology as a love monism, but then proceeded to develop a doctrine of reconciliation that provided no means of mediating between God's wrath and his love. Indeed, Ritschl denied the wrath of God as an Old Testament view of God. Herrmann counseled Christians deliberately to avoid seeking for a sense of God's wrath.[16]

Kitamori's *Theology of the Pain of God* first appeared shortly after the last war. Christians and non-Christians alike found it interesting. There is widespread feeling that both groups misread the book. In suffering themselves, they believed Kitamori was telling them that the Christian God suffered with them in their pain. This is not at all what he means, and obscures the most fascinating and novel element in Kitamori's position. The claim is made that " human pain is the expression of God's wrath," not the occasion for his compassion. What does Kitamori mean by that? Is he purveying the notion that God inflicts suffering as a punishment for sin? Yes, but only in the unusual sense that the suffering of mankind is an analogy, a symbol of the suffering God inflicts upon himself in the redemption of man.

Human pain is a symbol through which man is united to God. That is to say, the transcendent pain of God is immanent in the painful reality of the world.[17] Therefore the immanent pain must be taken as a clue to the transcendent pain. What else is the exegetical significance of the Herodian murder of infants in the Advent narrative? "In every year in which the church celebrates Christmas it fails to mention this painful event of the murder of babies, as if it were only accidental. The Bible considered it the fulfillment of prophecy (Jer. 31:15). . . . The parents of these children are witnesses to the pain of God and thus become the servants of God. The very meaninglessness of the whole event only increases the pain in it."[18] An exegesis of Matt., chs. 25 and 26, also illuminates the symbolic character of pain and is fairly characteristic of Kitamori's exegetical procedures. Matthew 25:31 ff. counsels the followers of Jesus to love their brothers, for God hides himself behind the reality of the neighbor. To love the neighbor is to love God. That is, God becomes immanent in the facts of human misery and the reality of pain. An act of love to God and an act of love to neighbor are like a shot at a target within a target. A single arrow can strike two targets in the same shot. Likewise, one act directed to the neighbor can simultaneously pertain to God.

How explain Matt. 26:6-13 in which Jesus condones an act of adoration toward himself that is evidently oblivious of responsibility toward the neighbor? The key to the passage is found in the verse in which it is made clear that Jesus is going to his death. When that is known, all else must be forgotten in the interests of concentrating on the fact of God's pain in the death of Jesus. It is permissible to forget all else in order to concentrate on this pain, because this is the pain that is immanent in all other pain, such as the pain of the neighbor. For at the base of all social misery is sin; and the pain of God in the forgiveness of sin is therefore immanent in all misery.[19]

The human willingness to bear pain becomes the symbolic witness to the pain of God. To follow Jesus, taking up one's own cross, is to bear pain as a witness. Here Kitamori seems to leave himself exposed to criticism. Is not the pain most people bear largely an expression of their own sin? Is not the pain over the loss of a child directly due to *erōs,* to self-interested love? Is it not when *erōs* is most strong that pain is most acute? The answer is already given in the question. The pain to which human pain is a witness is precisely the pain that is occasioned by embracing with love someone who does not deserve love. Thus the pain of man's sinful love becomes a symbol of and witness to the pain by which God's love overcomes sin.[20]

If there is any truth in Kitamori's understanding of the symbolic value of pain, some justification has at last been found for the existence of pain as an unresolved predicament. It is a witness to the pain of God. It is, in fact, a universal witness. Believers and unbelievers have a common basis in suffering. All suffering has the same origin in the alienation of man from God, and in the consequent wrath of God. But what is really symbolized in the suffering of man is the pain of God in which all suffering has its resolution, embracing the worthy and the unworthy alike. There is only one difference between the believer and the unbeliever. The believer realizes he is reconciled by the pain of

God. The unbeliever does not, and in his ignorance separates himself more and more from God when he experiences his pain. Yet that very condition of existing outside of God is a symbol of the pain of God who goes outside himself in Christ to reconcile men to himself. The believer has the responsibility of interpreting to the unbeliever the meaning of his pain by witnessing to the pain of God. Man's pain is a symbol not of punishment for his sin but of God's painful reconciliation of sin. To make the analogical transition from man's suffering to God's suffering is to shift from the problem of man's suffering to the problem of his sin, embraced by the painful love of God.[21]

The pain of God is not easy to understand in an age of joy. The Greek world and the modern world both stumbled over this truth. Although the truth is eternal, Kitamori fears it may lack a witness in the happy world of today.[22] Here lies the possible importance of Japan in theology today. For Japan, this has been largely an age of death and pain. Thus the Japanese Christians should be able to actualize the gospel of the pain of God by their witness. Luther thought he lived in a period of death because of the plague. When he emerged from the plague, he thought he lived in the golden age. There is more suffering now, Kitamori asserts, than Germany had in the sixteenth century. Hence, there is more opportunity to be sensitive to the gospel.

When an age is permeated by the problem of pain, the witness to God is strong. But when pain is driven away and joy is strong, where is the witness to God to be seen? Kitamori's answer has strong autobiographical overtones. "When the world is permeated with joy and one wishes to witness to pain, he becomes unavoidably an exception. The whole world is sustained by this particular individual."[23]

People in general may be allowed a happy life in God, but a few must live through the age of pain even in the age of joy. That is why Kitamori is willing to revive one of the leading ideas of monastic life. Obedience, poverty, hard work, fasting, and celibacy (Kitamori is a bachelor) can be understood as symbolic expressions of the age of pain even though occurring in the age of joy. The defect in monasticism was its search for suffering as an end in itself, reducing the discipline to what Karl Holl called "a pious game." For Kitamori, the disciplined life is a voluntary, active symbolization of the pain of God.[24]

Before taking up the second major aspect of Kitamori's work, namely, the effect of his interpretive principle upon the formulation of doctrines, two other factors may help to illuminate his position. One has to do with the Biblical base of his claims about the pain of God, and the other with its suitability to the Japanese way of thinking.

In the first place, critics of Kitamori indicate that his conclusions about the pain of God are not given in the Scriptures. If that be so, it is foreign to his intention, because, as he has said, "My theological thinking is to the end bound by the text."[25] What it means for Kitamori to be "bound by the text," however, has yet to be determined. It can be illustrated from his precarious theological controversy with a layman. Dr. Nobuo Odagiri, a Japanese physician who came into the Christian faith through the Y.M.C.A. movement, took issue with Kitamori's exegesis in a series of articles on the purported deity of Christ.[26] The New Testament does not support the theologian's claim that "Jesus is God," Odagiri asserted. Kitamori took the position against Odagiri that precise references to the deity of Christ are missing in the New Testament simply because that faith was the presupposition of the entire New Testament. One must not read the Bible by way of isolated verses. That would be roughly the equivalent of taking a census where encounter with a person is called for.[27] But if one insists on reading isolated verses, he should do so in the light of the whole Biblical tradition, not vice versa.

The same attitude is implicit in his handling of the Biblical basis of the theology of the pain of God. The New Testament is obviously cross-centered, and the cross is the event of God's painful forgiveness of sins. Kitamori's exegetical responsibility toward his doctrine is focused mainly on a series of Old Testament verses. The most pivotal is Jer. 31:20. Jeremiah is referred to as the Paul of the Old Testament, for Paul was determined to know nothing save the pain of God, and Jeremiah reveals a sympathetic anticipation of that position. Japan has now undergone three translations of the Bible. The version upon which Kitamori relies is the first revision that was the authorized version at the time he worked out his theology of the pain of God. According to it, Jer. 31:20 records God as saying, "I have pain in my bowels." Every occurrence of the Hebrew word *hāmāh* in the Old Testament manifests a single connotation, "pain." Luther's translation bears out Kitamori's understanding of the verse: "*Darum bricht mir mein Herz.*" Unfortunately, however, the third version, the colloquial translation of 1955, does not directly support Kitamori's project. "My heart yearns," it reads. The Japanese translation follows the Revised Standard Version in this. "What I have been warning against for twenty years," Kitamori writes in his 1958 revision of his classic book, "is now realized. The monism of divine love has been translated into the Bible." [28]

Kitamori accuses his critics of failing to confront the text theologically. The translation of the Bible is a confession of faith and not a mere linguistic achievement. Particular words in particular verses in the Bible must not be left with the meaning available through that simple location. They must be interpreted in the light of the tradition in which they are imbedded. Their broader significance, their theological sense, must be uncovered. Notwithstanding the paucity of precise passages pertaining to the pain of God, Kitamori believes he is doing nothing that Luther did not do with the concept of the hiddenness of God. When Luther came upon the words of Isa. 45:14, " Thou art a God who hidest thyself," he did not *base* his doctrine of *deus absconditus* upon that passage. Rather the passage became analogical to the broader theological significance of the hiddenness of God.[29]

In the next place, the correlation between the Christian understanding of the pain of God and the classical Japanese tradition is most instructive. It is believed that one can see the heart of the Japanese through their classical drama.[30] Japanese tragedy differs from the tragedy of other countries. Where Greek drama, for instance, developed tragedy on the basis of events or character, Japanese tragedy is developed upon human relations. The meaning of tragedy is present in one word, *tsurasa*. *Tsurasa* is the emotion that occurs when one kills himself or some loved one in order to let another live. It is the emotion of suffering, sorrow, or bitterness. The emotion becomes particularly contagious when it is restrained. Then the people can hear " the unexpressed sob," and they are moved. *Tsurasa* is translated into modern Japanese as " pain," and Kitamori regards it as a splendid analogy to the pain of God.

There is one important difference between *tsurasa* and the pain of God. In Japanese tragedy when one kills himself or a loved one to let another live, the life for which one sacrifices is always someone beloved. God's pain comes about, quite to the contrary, in loving one he cannot love and letting his Son die for the sake of that love. Japanese tragedy does not understand a love that loves the enemy. In that context, Western theologians are in a position to understand Kitamori's consternation over modern theology. The American theologian William Adams Brown is cited as saying: " God cannot give himself for an unworthy object. If then his redemptive love embraces the sinners and the outcast, it must be because he perceives in them the capacity of growth and manhood." [31] Hastings Rashdall, British theologian, is referred to as saying Hindus can be justified in so far as Christ can recognize their goodness.[32] As represented in these voices, modern theology has not retained the characteristic note of tragedy in the gospel, which is the pain of God in the act of loving those he ought not to love.

Another instance of correlation with classical Japanese motifs can be found in the Buddhist attitude toward suffering in God. In the sixth century, Shōtoku Taishi, a relative of the emperor, governed Japan while the emperor was young. He was responsible for introducing Buddhism into the country. He wrote a book called *Notes on the Yuimakyō*, the Buddhist scriptures. In the book he comments that " Buddhism's God of mercy has great sorrow because of the suffering of the people. Why? It is explained this way: illness is saved by illness. The God of mercy has an illness because of his desire to save others from illness." Kitamori cites this story in order to say, " I am happy to find a thought in our tradition from Buddhism that is very close to the truth." Where does it fall short of the truth? At the point of the pain of God. Buddhism lacks wrath in its absolute. Thus the sorrow and suffering of Buddhism is only sympathy, and not pain.

The situation that Kitamori's doctrine faces in Japan,

therefore, is highly paradoxical. Theoretically, Buddhism should not emphasize pain in its absolute, but actually in its expression in Japan it does so. Contrariwise, Christianity should emphasize the pain of God theoretically, but in its actual manifestation in the modern theology by which Japan has known Christianity, the note of pain in God has been deficient.[33]

II

"The theology of the pain of God" is meant for the most serious theological consideration. It is not just one doctrine among doctrines. For Kitamori it is the doctrine at the base of the doctrines. It is the prolegomenon for dogmatics. "Dogmatics is the form of thinking concerned with the problem of pain in God as the primary interest."[34]

One might ask if so passionate a category is not a bit out of character for a Japanese theologian, the Japanese being a traditionally reserved people. Kitamori answers that query by referring to the Notes of Norinaga Motoori upon the *Kojiki*, Book 27. According to these notes, the ancient hero of Japan is a man who could be brave when necessary and sorrowful when necessary. Not only reserve, therefore, but the expression of sorrow is a Japanese virtue.[35]

One might ask further if so passionate a category as pain is not a bit out of character for a theologian whose craft seems to call for *logos* and not *pathos*. Kitamori's response to that is to say that while theology is a *logos*, it is a *logos* concerned with a *pathos*, namely, the pain of God. Hence, it is the task of the *logos* to conserve the *pathos*. Logic is the way one handles things. To treat the *pathos* of God's pain in the *logos* of theology is, in the last analysis, an impossibility. Therefore, the theology of the pain of God "has the fatal destiny of being a failure in the end. If we succeed in making *pathos* logical, our success is in reality failure. Why, then, assume a task that is fated to fail? Because salvation is a matter of *pathos* and salvation must be communicated. This can be done only through the medium of *logos*. Hence, the burning flame of *pathos* must be controlled by *logos*." [36] Closely associated with that position is an even more plaintive claim. Kitamori believes that a theology of pain can only really establish itself *through* pain. The peculiar path of the theology of pain will be that it must keep the character of an outsider. It can never be the dominant theology of the church. It must become " the refuse of the world " in order to remain true to itself.[37]

The truth is that the theology of the pain of God has become popular among the Christians of Japan, though not among the academic theologians. The popularity seems justifiable, if only by virtue of the way in which Kitamori has been able to demonstrate the hermeneutical function of doctrine. The doctrines of the church are designed to illuminate human experience and to conserve the meanings that illuminate. It is a fascinating exercise in Christian understanding to see how Kitamori makes some of the traditionally forbidding doctrines come alive with meaning, albeit the meaning of the pain of God.

The doctrine of the analogy of being (*analogia entis*) traditionally has meant that there are in the created world positive clues to the truth of God. Kitamori now attempts to supplant the method of reasoning from created being by what he calls the analogy of pain (*analogia doloris*). Roman Catholicism, which is the chief locus of the method of *analogia entis*, is right in its method in so far as theological thinking involves positive knowledge about God, although only analogically positive. However, the weakness of this method is its failure to show how the disruption effected by sin is overcome. How can a man who is living in disobedience toward God come to know God apart from God's redemptive mediation? The *analogia doloris*, on the other hand, is analogy not in the order of creation but in the order of redemption. The acts in which the knowledge of God is given are the very acts in which the disobedience of man is overcome, through the pain of God.[38]

If " the pain of God " is the basic form of all doctrine and if the *analogia doloris* is the method of thinking doctrinally, then traditional Christian doctrines that have not adopted these methods stand to be revised in some sense. Up to this point, Kitamori has given only hints as to how his prolegomenon would work itself out in Christian doctrine. Whether he will ever proceed to a full-scale dogmatics in the same way Kumano has is very doubtful. He seems dispositionally predisposed against that method. The lines that he has already proposed, however, are significant in themselves and should be given attention by theologians both inside and outside Japan. What follows here are mere intimations of what a dogmatics might look like if constructed on the foundation of such a prolegomenon.

What the *analogia doloris* does to the doctrine of the Trinity seems most revolutionary. Probably it is revolutionary chiefly to those who, like Karl Barth, have espoused an immanental view of the Trinity. This is the view of the Trinity that defines God's threeness in terms of relations within the Godhead. God is Father in respect of generating the Son, Son in respect of filiating with the Father, and Holy Spirit in respect of the breath of love that flows between the Father and the Son. If the essence of God is pain, however, then the immanental doctrine of the Trinity misses the most essential thing about God. God the Father is not simply the being who gives birth to the Son. He is the being who lets the Son die. Generating the Son is simply secondary background to sacrificing the Son. It is the task of the doctrine of the Trinity today, therefore, to bring the cross of Christ back inside God's existence.[39]

The task of a Christology is corollary to the task of a doctrine of the Trinity. The function of the doctrine of the Trinity in Kitamori's concept is to include the work of Christ, the Son, within the divine economy. The function of the doctrine of the incarnation is to show how the work of Christ is also outside the Godhead. Indeed, it is the very meaning of Christ that he is "the God who goes out of God, to save the humanity which is of God." [40] A complete Christology must conserve two dimensions in one person: the outsideness of God, which is his pain, and the insideness of God, which is the divine reality of pain.

The formulas that have neglected one or the other side of this dualism are the traditional Christological and Trinitarian heresies. Modalistic monarchianism emphasized the sameness in God at the expense of his otherness and differentiation. If God is not differentiated, he cannot go outside himself, and hence his pain, which is his outsideness, has no ground in his being. Dynamic monarchianism emphasized the otherness of God while making no room for his sameness. Consequently, while it allowed for the pain of separation, it did not show how that pain could be God's own pain. The reader should now be prepared for one of the most cryptic yet revealing sentences in the Kitamori literature: "The pain of God is nothing but the outsideness of God's selfsameness." [41]

Arianism was a form of dynamic monarchianism that conserved the outsideness in indifference to the selfsameness of God. According to Arius, the Son is outside God but not as God. The Son is outside God only as the first creature. It was right, therefore, that Athanasius should vanquish Arius at Nicea, for Athanasius, although agreeing that the Father, Son, and Holy Spirit are different, nevertheless conserved their sameness in the word *homoousion.* By that highly debated word he saved the theology of the pain of God for the church.[42] That word is now taken by Kitamori to mean that the event of the incarnation is related to the essence of God; the cross is the cross of this incarnate one; therefore, the cross of this incarnate one is related to the essence of God. "This fact," he says, "I call the pain of God."[43] Modern theology is in the tradition of Arianism because it has allowed Christ to lose his *essential* position. In modern theology, God's love in Christ is essentially the same as God's love without Christ. Hence, there is a real connection between the denial of *homoousion* and the denial of pain in God.[44]

Docetism is the opposite heresy from Arianism. Docetism traditionally has meant that, in Christ, God only *seemed* to be fully man. According to the Christian faith, however, God *really* entered history and bore *real* sin. Sin is that which should not be forgiven. The pain of God means the forgiving of sin that should not be forgiven. Docetism, therefore, would involve an abstract concept of sin, a concept that does not involve God in pain.[45]

Only with this Trinitarian and Christological background is it possible to see why Kitamori refuses to concede that he is a Patripassian. He does not commit the Patripassian heresy, at least not in the form in which it was first branded a heresy. Patripassianism is not the simple claim that God the Father suffers. Patripassianism is based upon modalistic monarchianism, which makes no distinction between Father and Son. In modalistic monarchianism, therefore, the sufferings of the Son and the sufferings of the Father are identical.

Kitamori rejects this position for two reasons. The first is the customary Trinitarian reason. In the death of Christ, God does not become nothing. He lives on in the person of the Father. God goes outside himself only in the person of the Son. What one says of the Son he cannot therefore equally say of the Father. This fact of the pain of God was obscured in Patripassianism because of its monarchian view of the Trinity based only on sameness in God.[46]

The second reason Kitamori has for rejecting Patripassianism is even more closely related to what he means by the pain of God. The pain of God is that God goes outside himself. But in Patripassianism there is no outsideness, for modalistic monarchianism admits of no real differentiation within the Godhead. If there is no outsideness in Patripassianism, then paradoxically neither is there pain in God, at least not in the sense in which Kitamori means it. In Patripassianism, the one who suffers on the cross is the Father himself. In Kitamori's view the suffering of the cross is the division within God in which the Father allows the Son to go outside the Godhead, to die. "The moment of outsideness distinguishes the theology of pain from Patripassianism." [47] "In Patripassianism, there is no distinction between the first and second Persons of the Trinity. It is the Father who is suffering in the Son, therefore there is no *bunretsu*, no pain of division." [48]

In a theology built on the *analogia doloris* it is quite evident that the Lutheran tradition dominates. Soteriology becomes formative of the whole of theology. Trinity and Christology tend to become doctrinal safeguards for the methodologically more central concern, salvation. Thus it is instructive to see the conclusions Kitamori draws for a doctrine of atonement. Which of the traditional types best conserves the meaning of the pain of God? In his collection of essays called *The Character of the Gospel* he has treated the question with ingenuity in the leading essay written in 1947 and called simply " Atonement." This essay elaborates Kitamori's view in relation to two popular positions, the one taken by the Swedish theologian Gustav Aulén in his little work, *Christus Victor*, and the one taken by Kōkichi Kurosaki, a leader in the Non-Church movement in Japan.

The main contribution of Aulén's position, as far as Kitamori is concerned, is the way it criticizes the traditional satisfaction theory of the atonement sponsored by the medieval theologian Anselm. According to Anselm, in dealing with man's sin, God's love is hindered by his righteousness. God's love can freely operate only after his righteousness is satisfied. God's atoning deed in Christ is therefore a legal, rational, logical compromise with God's righteousness in order to release his love. Kitamori agrees with Aulén that the satisfaction theory lacks a certain furiousness, a certain passionate quality. Aulén supplies this in his understanding of atonement as a *conflict* between God's love and his wrath in which love is the *victor*. Kitamori cannot reject that view; he can only stop short of its conclusion. The atonement for Kitamori's theology is not so much in the victory as it is in the conflict. The conflict is the pain of God.

The penal theory of atonement, or, as it is better known, the substitutionary theory, asserts that God puts the sins of man upon Christ as a substitute for mankind. It is Christ who in his crucifixion receives the punishment of God that might justifiably have been directed against men as sinners. Kitamori concedes that there is more Biblical and existential (*sic*) support for this theory than for the satisfaction theory. But Kurosaki is supported in criticizing it as being too mechanical and impersonal. God is no impersonal judge who keeps a ledger on man's deeds. There is something more passionate and warm in the atoning deed. Kurosaki abandons this theory too soon, however, when he prefers a moral-influence theory instead. In the penal theory, God directs his wrath against Christ who bears that wrath for men. In the moral-influence theory, Jesus bore the sins of man as an elder brother substitutes for the sins of a younger brother. Jesus suffered for sins that were not his own as if they were his own. Deeply moved by Jesus' self-sacrifice, God forgives man's sins. The weakness in the theory for Kitamori is that there is no moment of wrath involved, hence no moment of pain in God. There is pathos in the theory, and suffering, but without God's wrath, without his self-separation, that suffering is only sentimental. The pain, which is the synthesis of love and wrath, is absent.

The fundamental structure of the atoning act that Kitamori proposes as an alternative to these traditional views is found by him in Rom. 3:21 ff. The righteousness of God apart from the law is manifested in Christ. According to the law, in order to save God's position as righteous, man's position as sinner would have to be destroyed. But if one were to try to save man's position, God's would be destroyed. A righteous God ought not to love a sinner. According to the law, there is a fundamental either/or that says God and man cannot both stand. But Jesus Christ is the righteousness *apart* from the law. In him the either/or is overcome by a both/and. Through Christ, God can remain righteous because man is declared righteous. Both positions can stand together. This is " the character of the gospel " that stands against the law.

How does this shift from dialectical contradiction to dialectical combination come about? That is the heart of the atonement in the theology of the pain of God. In the cross, Christ is forsaken by both God and man in the perfect solitude of neither/nor. At Golgotha the Jews and the Romans forsake Christ, and the common man cries for his execution. At this moment Christ appeals to the Father, " Why hast *thou* forsaken me? " Trying to save God's righteousness, Christ is forsaken of God, and trying to justify man's position, he is forsaken of men. " Transcending the either/or of the law, and attempting to bring about the both/and of reconciliation, he placed himself in the neither/nor of absolute solitude. That is the deepest meaning of pain. The way of Christ as redeemer is the *via dolorosa*." [49]

The doctrine of the atonement immediately involves theology in two related doctrines, the church and ethics. The reason for this consequence is that " the pain of the redeemer immediately demands the pain of the believer." [50] The church, then, is the continuing witness to the pain of God through its own pain, and ethics is the service of the pain of God in the service of the pain of others. It now remains to show how the theme of " the pain of God " affects the elaboration of these two doctrines.

The church is the clearest symbol of the pain of God. The one place in reality where the pain of the cross continues to appear by virtue of Christian responsibility is the church. Each believer is assigned the role of suffering servant.[51] Those who are reconciled through Christ have his ministry of reconciliation to the world. (II Cor. 5:19.) The ministry is achievable only through the pain of disruption in a man's own existence. Paul the apostle is the prototype for this costly form of discipleship. The problem of disruption between Christian and Jew, for instance, was faced by Paul. The Jews as a people had repudiated Christ, yet Paul as a Christian could not cease being a Jew. He loved the Jews and maintained solidarity with them. At the same time, he could not separate himself from Christ. He was to the end both a Christian and a Jew. Embracing both in one, Paul experienced the pain of disruption as an instrument of reconciliation.[52] In the same pattern of apostleship "the church must accept solidarity with the world, embracing what ought not to be embraced. This is its cross." [53] Kitamori seems to relish his quotation from an American scholar to the effect that "[the Suffering Servant's] admirers then, as now, were probably many, his followers few." [54]

Just as evidently the church must accept solidarity with other churches. For Kitamori, ecumenicity is not necessarily the recognition by one church of the gospel truth in the other churches from which it may be divided. He simply calls for an ecumenicity on the basis of obedience to the gospel truth that is within one's own church. That gospel truth means the embracing of what ought not to be embraced. Ecumenicity in Kitamori's view is not a simple solution to the division of the churches. It is divertingly based, not upon witness to oneness in Christ when that oneness does not exist in actuality, but is based upon witness to the pain of God, whose suffering love embraces what ought not be embraced. If Luther and Zwingli had understood that at Marburg, they would never have felt compelled to divide over what they believed to be a fundamental question of truth. Notwithstanding the truth question involved in the doctrine of the sacraments, they could have remained together on the basis of the more fundamental truth of the gospel, which is the truth that what ought not to be embraced can be embraced. Churches that recognize only the immutability of their divisions sponsor sectarianism. Churches that recognize only the tragedy of their divisions become sentimental ecumenicist, contributing to the existence of a latitudinarian church. The gospel calls the church to a witness to the pain of God. That witness does not require differences to be resolved in advance of reconciliation.[55]

The atonement of Christ, which extends itself in the reconciling existence of the church, also extends itself through the witness of the Christian's ethical obedience. Those who live in the church live in the age of pain. Therefore, the ethics of the church should be an ethics of pain. The ethical service of a Christian, however, is not just any sort of self-sacrifice. It is the particular form of sacrificial service to others in which the pain of God is expressed. Real love to the neighbor is suffering love because one feels another's suffering as one's own. How is this to be achieved? Only through being in the pain of God ourselves and knowing the pain of others as in the pain of God. Only in this way, of course, is ethical behavior in any way related to the atoning deed. For human pain has a deeper reality than appears on the surface. What remains when the problem of poverty, for instance, is solved? Sin remains. Ethical acts are therefore those acts which serve the neighbor in his profoundest need, that is, in his need for reconciliation.[56] The essence of the pain of God is that it embraces opposites, such as the opposites of love and wrath. The essence of practical behavior based upon the pain of God, therefore, would virtually be "a prayer for peace."[57]

It would be difficult to recall anyone in Western Protestantism of whom it can be said more truly than of Kitamori that the human imagination has been placed at the disposal of theology. The question now remains as to whether he will follow the precedent set by Luther himself, a precedent so characteristic of contemporary European Lutherans. Will he content himself with developing theological essays, not taking the trouble to construct a systematic theology? Or will he one day write the dogmatics implicit in " the theology of the pain of God "? Can it be said of Kitamori as Seiichi Hatano once said of his famous pupil, Kiyoshi Miki, that he is too imaginative to be systematic? If that is so, will it be interpreted, as Hatano seems to have meant it, as a limitation rather than a strength, as if creative imagination and disciplined construction were ultimately at odds? In the case of a theologian who is still in his early forties, there is no real urgency about an answer to that line of questioning.

IV | *The Theology of the Time of Love*

WITHOUT LOVE, HUMAN LIFE IS AN IRREVERSIBLE DRIFT TOward death. That, in short, is the position of the most learned Christian in the one hundred years of Japanese Protestantism, Seiichi Hatano, late professor of Christianity at the University of Kyoto. For Hatano, eternity is the time of love, and theology is the exposition of that time. What Hatano means is that life is time. But time is continually running out. How, then, can a man realize himself when he is destined to live under conditions that are continually threatened by mortality? One way is to use others as props by which to stabilize his own unsteady reality. Humanity seems to have chosen that way. The history of human culture is, therefore, the history of just such an effort. There is irony in that approach, however. For human existence is stable only in the presence of others, others who are real in themselves and not simply artifacts of a man's own program of self-realization. Making others the object of his own use suppresses their reality, hence undercuts the supportive fellowship apart from which man perishes.

Consequently, a man can only truly be himself who allows to others a reality of their own. What is allowed to be real in itself thereafter becomes the source of his own reality. The Christian symbols reveal just such a structure in reality. According to the Christian symbols, God, by appearing in Christ as love, defines his own being as real. The real otherness of God is what provides the foundation that prevents human time from slipping into nothingness and death. This very love of God transforms temporality into eternity. That, in short, is Hatano's fully developed theology.

The details of how Hatano himself became a Christian and how he pursued his vocation as a Christian illuminate some of the distinctive elements in his theological result. While studying at the University of Tokyo he attended the church whose minister was one of Japan's most suggestive Christian interpreters, Masahisa Uemura, a theologian in the Reformed tradition. His baptism into the Christian faith at the hands of Uemura was also, therefore, a commitment to the rigorous intellectual appropriation of the faith.

Hatano's academic discipline took the form of research into the Western sources of modern philosophy. The immediate outcome was what Japanese scholars regard as the first thoroughgoing work in the history of Western philosophy to be written in Japanese. The Christian bearing of this technical research is not so obvious until it is known to what conclusion the study led Hatano. The root of Western thought, he found, was in Christianity. Thus an evident circularity entered his scholarship. His Christian faith had given him a vocation to the rigorous investigation of Western philosophy. Western philosophy in turn led him to a disciplined investigation of the historical sources of the Christian faith. The enormous prestige he attracted for his classical and Christian scholarship made it possible for the

University of Kyoto to offer him the first professorship in the Christian religion to be established in a state university of Japan.

In the light of Hatano's rich contribution to Christian thinking, it seems purely academic to argue that he was not a theologian. Japanese philosophers seem willing to concede that he was a theologian when they deplore the fact that his appointment to a professorship in Christian studies robbed Japanese philosophy of a first-class historian. His careful investigation of Western philosophy, they claim, might have changed "the map of modern Japanese philosophy." [1] Yet, theologians tend to locate Hatano with the philosophers and with those philosophers of religion who deal with Christianity at an objective distance, elaborating its essence in relation to religion in general rather than to Christianity in particular.[2]

It seems utterly captious not to embrace the work of Hatano as plainly serious theology. The least one can say is that it is philosophical theology or philosophy of religion. But even as philosophy of religion it resists classification. Although it is structured by the concepts of Western philosophy, it is avowedly dependent upon the Christian faith. In the midst of his book entitled *Philosophy of Religion*, Hatano openly confesses what should have been obvious anyway, that his key category, *agapē*, has been derived from his study of primitive Christianity.[3] Again, it is axiomatic in his philosophy of religion that the first step in the direction of right understanding of religion is experience, and that experience in religion involves taking a position from within some concrete religion. Hatano's devotion to Christianity did not follow the pattern of the ordinary churchman. But no one was left in doubt about his identification with the Christian faith. When the *Philosophy of*

Religion appeared, Prof. Shōgo Yamaya, New Testament scholar at Tokyo Union Theological Seminary, called it a work of philosophy with no relation to Christian studies. Hatano rejected that evaluation with the protest that " my philosophy of religion is grounded in the New Testament and stands upon it." Some force is added to Hatano's claim when it is known that this interchange was first revealed by Professor Yamaya himself, in his address at Hatano's burial.

Hatano's philosophy of religion is Christian apologetics of the most subtle and sophisticated variety, the variety best suited to the Japanese spirit. I mean to say that its subtlety is not contrived but inheres in its sophistication. Hatano does not set out to convert the Japanese to Christianity. He sets out to contribute to Japanese philosophy the metaphysical profundities that are revealed through the Christian faith. He does so in the conviction which he developed in his observation of the correlation of Christianity and Western philosophy. Religion, he concludes, is the soul and source of all metaphysics. " All religion contains metaphysics within itself. Philosophy, which derives from one's consciousness of the world, should have a connection with religion if it is to be real metaphysics." [4] Martin Heidegger has taken the position, for instance, that the philosophy of Aristotle is mainly ontology. Hatano concedes that this is true of the later works of Aristotle. He claims, however, that the earlier works were not ontology but theology, and that for Aristotle theology had priority not only over ontology but over all the other branches of science. Hatano believes Aristotle caught this suggestion for the priority of theology from Plato.

As a result of Hatano's teaching and writing, the Christian faith has become a live option for an important sector of the Japanese populace, namely, those who are always ready to dismiss Christianity as Westernism and missionary intrusiveness. Even more important, he has contributed to world Christianity a rigorously systematic and comprehensive account of the faith from within, expressed in a brief and beautiful literature, and carefully co-ordinated to the one word to which the apostle Paul himself was willing to reduce the Christian faith, to " love " (Gal. 5:14).

Japanese scholars disagree on the status of Hatano in the future development of Christian thought in Japan. Some feel a Hatano renaissance is imminent. " There will come a time," Professor Yamaya has said, " when to read the complete works of Hatano . . . will be the first duty of the Japanese theologian." [5] Others believe Hatano can have no serious impact upon contemporary Japan because he did not significantly take into account the more vital spirit of such currently influential figures as Kierkegaard, Dostoevsky, and Barth. He was critical of Heidegger and Barth, whereas the present generation prefers Heidegger and Barth and identifies Hatano with an earlier generation.

Hatano's personality and his style do seem to typify the prewar mode. His insight, however, even in the setting of current Japanese thinking, is advanced. One would not realize this who had not struggled with his latest work, *Time and Eternity*. There it can be seen how classical, Biblical, and existential categories come together in a study of time and being. This theme is in the forefront of current theological and philosophical discussion, and what Hatano contributes to its development merits a hearing.

Time and Eternity pursues the thesis that the structure of the time in which one lives is directly qualified by the type of love in which one lives.[6] Different qualities of love characterize each of three stages on life's way.

Natural life is the time of desire (*epithumia*) where the future moves unchecked through the present into the nothingness of the past. Cultural life is the time of *erōs* where past and future seem sucked up by the present, that vampire of self-realization. Religious life is the time of *agapē* where fellowship with the trustworthy otherness of God is a future that saves the present from slipping into the nothingness of the past.

Tripartite schemes of this sort are not strange to Western thinkers. Kierkegaard's aesthetic, ethical, and religious " stages " are surely suggested in Hatano's scheme, and an excellent access to Kierkegaard's thinking was given the Japanese as early as 1917 when Prof. Tetsuo Watsuji published his careful work. However, there seems to be no evidence that Hatano was directly dependent upon Kierkegaard. In Hatano one might more easily find Hegel's dialectical pattern of movement from thesis to antithesis to synthesis, especially considering the interweaving of the categories of love and time in Hegel's thought. Schleiermacher's three levels of relation of the self to an other are almost identical to Hatano's structure. The level of the flesh, where the self senses its complete domination over the other, parallels what Hatano calls the natural life. The level of the soul, where the self and the other exist in mutual interdependence, parallels the cultural life. And the highest level, the level of the spirit, where the self senses its absolute dependence upon the other, answers to Hatano's description of the religious life. The only parallels to his scheme which Hatano explicitly acknowledges, however, are Dante's movement from inferno through purgatory to paradise, and Pascal's movement from the level of body through spirit to love.[7]

Hatano's doctrinal formulations are directly related to

his account of the temporal structure of existence. Therefore, it seems best to consider his Christian beliefs in the setting of these three stages and to show how one stage is believed to lead to another by a kind of dialectical law of life.

1. *Natural life is the time of desire.* By " natural " Hatano means what Greek philosophy presumably meant: the simple, direct being as contrasted with the artificial being. In natural life the self is in a direct relationship with others. Direct relationships with others are relations of immediacy, however, in which the sense of the otherness of others is deficient. This unreflective immersion in others, weak in the sense of otherness, is the very source of temporality and of the oppressive characteristics of human experience that open the consciousness of the self to higher levels of life.

" Temporality " means something vastly different for Hatano from the common-sense preoccupation with calendar time. " Temporality " is the time man experiences, and must be distinguished from the objective time that is time as man records it and speculates about it. Objective time has very little bearing upon man's selfhood. Philosophy, therefore, is basically concerned with moving beyond the consideration of objective time to time as it is actually experienced. In experienced time there are three dimensions, each of which affects a man's very being in a unique way. The present is defined as the reality that is contributing to his being. In experienced time, the present is the true existence, the true selfhood. There, life is full of content and dynamic. Outside the present, there is no real life. The past is the reality that is depriving one of being. The past keeps the present in flux, always draining the dynamic of life into its vacuum, which is nothingness. The past is the present in the mode of its disappearance. It is the experience of annihilation. The future is what comes into the present, as opposed to the past, which is the present in its dwindling away. As such, the future is the mediating agency between past and present, the very source of a present that is otherwise continually only passing into the past. The future, then, is not simply the time that has "not yet come" (for which the Japanese have the word *mirai*). The future is the time that constitutes our very present because it is "about to come," giving the present a reality it would not have without the future (for which the Japanese have the word *shōrai*). What has "not yet come" has no more status than the past. It is itself a kind of non-being. What is "about to come" is some being that will replace the present being, which is drifting into the non-being of the past. The future as *shōrai*, therefore, has an ontological status not enjoyed by the future as *mirai*. "In Japanese philosophy," Hatano has said, "people usually mix these words without thinking. We must be careful to distinguish them." [8]

The similarities with Augustine's deeply psychological understanding of time are evident to Hatano. Bergson is also in his thinking, for Bergson, like Hatano, distinguished the technological time, which measures the discontinuous spaces of time, from the experienced time through which man continuously lives. Hatano is right to indicate, however, that neither Augustine nor Bergson saw the future as the mediator between past and present.[9] Although Hatano does not say so, in contemporary philosophy it was Martin Heidegger who first showed what seemed to be implicit in the Biblical faith from the beginning. Heidegger sponsored the view that time is a concept in which the future has a unique precedence over both present and past. For Hatano as for Heidegger, in time "the center of gravity is always on the side of the future," the future as *shōrai*.[10]

The time of natural life, then, is not simply a movement in a linear direction from the past through the present to the future. It is an irreversible movement into the past. It is a movement from being to nothingness, from present to past, from the being that the present enjoys at the hands of the future to a nothingness that is the past. Temporality in this sense is synonymous with instability and corruptibility. Being in this kind of lived time is a being in want. There is no other alternative. Man has no choice about the fact of temporality. It is his fate. To be is not to be. To become is to perish. One cannot expect to realize the meaning of life under these conditions. Everything ends in a dream. " In temporality there is always the negation of the meaning of life, a want of happiness, a feeling of emptiness and uneasiness, and solitude." [11]

The sense of the perishability of present time first arises in natural life in the relation with others. The reality of others is what supplies a man with the content and possibility of his own reality. Yet, at the same time, the very existence of others threatens his own existence with extinction. What Hatano sketches with almost ascetic philosophical brevity, the French existentialists, Sartre and Camus, have expanded in a voluminous literature. According to Camus, life is a process of " cross purposes " in which reality fails to support our projects, reducing life to an absurdity worthy only of revolt. That is why for Camus suicide is the major philosophical problem. Suicide is a method of revolt against an otherwise meaningless universe. The fact that, in Japan, Camus is the most widely read existentialist is not, therefore, mysterious. According to Sartre, moreover, life is a tension brought on by the " look " that others direct at us. " Without a looker-on, a man evaporates," yet by a look one man may annihilate another. The desires of others decentralize a man's own existence. He feels a sense of " lack " when his own reality is suddenly negated by the intentions in the " look " of others.

Hatano poses the irony of existence in much the same way as these existentialists do. " Hell is other people " for Sartre and the natural life for Hatano is comparable to Dante's inferno. But there is one important difference between Hatano and the existentialists. The irony of the existentialists probes no deeper than a fate that man cannot penetrate, and the irony is relieved only by acts of heroism in the face of irremediable meaninglessness. The irony of Hatano is a revelation of mechanisms by which a man may see he has fabricated the very fates that thwart him. That self-knowledge opens up a hope that transcends the courage man has in the presence of his fate. The courage of a possible faith is made available.

According to Hatano's analysis, an individual's sense of support in existence is an attribute of his immediate relations with others, others who are real in themselves. The very immediacy of the relationship tempts him to neglect the concrete reality of others, making them objects of his own assertiveness. Man enjoys himself by making others his object, his property, the means of his livelihood. In this act he commits a kind of suicide, however, for his own existence actually depends upon the being of a reality distinct from himself. Independent realities relate to man as a future (*shōrai*) which is always coming toward him, saving his presentness from slipping into the past. However, in reducing others to objects of desire, he drives them into the past where they lose their capacity to insure his own present.[12]

This, then, is the irony of the natural life: other selves

supply us with the possibility of our existence. Other selves also threaten us with annihilation by organizing life around themselves. Natural man is the being who asserts himself against others in order to avert their threat to him. In the process he cuts off the possibility that others supply for his very existence. The mechanisms that humanity thereafter invents by which to cope with the self-defeating tactics of natural life are what Hatano knows as cultural life.

2. *Cultural life is the time of* erōs. *Erōs* is a method of liberating the self from the assertion of others who threaten its own reality. The strategy of *erōs* is to dissolve the concrete reality of individual others into a buffer zone of mediation in which the individual reality of others is neutralized and the threat to a man's own individuality is suspended. The life in which this device is pursued is variously called " human " or " historical " life, but the standard term for Hatano is " cultural " life. The word for " culture " is *bunka*. Hatano seems to use a play on words to fix his point, for *bunka* sounds the same as another word meaning " to separate," and culture does just that. Culture facilitates the coexistence of selves by interrupting and curtaining off the immediacies of natural life.

The main motif in cultural life is the absorption of others into the orbit of a man's own self-realization. He uses another as the mediator for his own self-realization. Fellowship based on this device is known as *erōs*. In such relations, others lose the status of concrete reality. They become mere attributes of other selves. They become secondary or vestigial selves. " In *erōs* the subject will expand into infinity, so that finally all existence in the world will be involved in the self, and the outwardness, the basic spatiality between the self and others, is seemingly overcome." [13]

A corollary of this motif is in the way in which selves

make themselves available for absorption by other selves through self-expression. The natural life has prepared for the cultural life in this regard. Natural life is a dialogue between independent realities, but the words used in the dialogue acquire a mediatorial function that breaks down the characteristic immediacy of natural life. Verbal expression takes on the aspect of a third person, a mediator, and that indirect form of being is what Hatano means by culture.[14]

Furthermore, when the self expresses itself in meanings, it compromises its center and independence. Here is another irony. The world of reality cannot exist without expressing itself; but when it does, it loses its independence. It transmutes its reality into an ideality that lacks a center of independence by virtue of the very openness to others that makes the expression effective. Self-expression makes the self observable by all, but only as an object of contemplation.

The success of the cultural life is best observed in the way in which cultural time transforms natural time. The perishing present of natural time is superseded in cultural time by "permanent presentness." [15] But where there is no perishing of the present into the past, there is no nonbeing. Cultural life appears, therefore, where only being prevails. For one who is filled with *erōs*, a moment of time will mean an eternity. Everything is possessed by *erōs*, including the past and the future. Therefore the present can be enjoyed. "The temporal aspect of cultural life is expressed only as present. The subject never bemoans the disappearing past or complains about the coming future. He simply enjoys the present in which he lives." [16] Past and future are only the inner structure of presentness. The past is the content of recollection. Being, which natural time once reduced to nothingness by allowing it to slip into the past, is resurrected by cultural time in an act of recall. Natural time moves from being to nothing. Cultural time moves from the nothingness of the past to its being in the present of cultural enjoyment. Likewise, imagination does for the future what recollection does for the past.

What is the defect in cultural life? It is the same defect that appeared at the level of natural life. The effort of the self to absorb other selves into its own program of self-realization is tantamount to " digging its own grave." [17] The real content of the world consists in community between persons, variously called " society," " history," and " morality." True community cannot be preserved at the cultural level where independent personal realities are reduced to epiphenomena of a man's own erotic goals.

Another defect more directly related to the unique elements of the cultural life is the experience of what Hegel called the " bad infinity." Cultural life prides itself on its permanent presentness. It is one long homogeneous " now." Where that is so, how does one distinguish one " now " from another? In permanent presentness there is no beginning and no end, and no criterion by which to judge one moment superior to another. Under such questioning, the sheer endlessness that one observes in cultural time cannot be confused with eternity. We do not really live in this time. We only see it. There our being always remains only in its possibility, never actualizing itself. What reveals itself in the objective world as endlessness, or permanent presentness, is actually a structure of " incompleteness, fragmentariness, and instability." It is not a conquering of time but a prolongation of the defects of time.[18]

These negative disclosures which appear in temporality at the cultural level are called death. Culture protracts time and calls it eternity without solving the problem of death.

Death is the symbol that opens the possibility of a higher than cultural stage of life. Death in the tragic sense could not have appeared in the natural stage of life, for there only isolated moments vanished into the past. In cultural life these same moments are dominated by the erotic assimilation of all reality into the present. When death threatens cultural life, therefore, it threatens the whole of life. Death in this sense is quite a different symbol from death in the mind of the primitive man who viewed death simply as an extension of life. That notion can be completely accommodated to cultural existence. Nor is death in this total sense to be confused with the Buddhist view of death. Buddhism solves death by a notion of reincarnation. However, Buddhism actually does not think of death but only of the continuation of life, which is a kind of cultural accommodation of the symbol of death.

Death in the tragic sense cuts off the relation between the self and others. But others represent the very possibility of our future. With death, the future disappears in its fundamental significance.[19] To be a self without an other is to have a life without a future. Such a present loses its existence to the past. To have a future means to have the opportunity to be with others. But "when this taproot of existence is cut off and the self is left by itself, it has no alternative but to wither away into nonbeing." Death is that sort of complete, thoroughgoing destruction of the self.[20]

Hatano knows of only two solutions to the tragedy of death. One is to overcome time in death, the other is to overcome death in time. The first is the way of the Buddhist *gedatsu*, which is the destruction of the self. The second is the Christian way, which relates the self to time, the time of love, which is eternity. Eternity is the present, which has no past, only a future. Death is the complete *gedatsu*, the being cut off from others. Eternity is complete coexistence of life with others. Death is isolation and solitude. Eternity can only be interpreted as community in love.[21] *Erōs*, as Plato's *Symposium* makes plain, is love ascending from man in hope of self-fulfillment through union with the very essence of things. Death cuts the thread of that hope when it separates us from the reality apart from which we have no future. There is another love, however. It is the love that Dante's *Divine Comedy* delineates through Beatrice. This is no love where everything simply ascends. Is not this lady the grace of God " coming down " to draw man up to Himself, and is not this love different from the *erōs* of Plato's *Symposium*? [22] The primitive church called it *agapē*, and Hatano finds eternity to be the ultimate hope of human life because it is the time of *agapē*.

3. *Religious life is the time of agapē*. The time in which the past of death is overcome by a fellowship of love is called eternity. Love as *agapē* is love as a fellowship with a real other. Religion occurs where the past of death is overcome by fellowship with the reality and otherness of God.

Natural time was a realm of corruptibility where everything was constantly slipping into the past, into death. Cultural time was a permanent present, but permanent only in the sense of a protracted delay of death through the exploitation of others as mediators. Religious time is a present that is conserved, not by being endlessly protracted as in culture, but by being in relation to a real other, an other that by nature resists becoming the instrument of cultural devices. Where the real otherness of God touches our perishable time, time is converted into eternity. Eternity overcomes the death of the past through this fellowship of love. Our future is in the attitude of expecting the presence of God, the fellowship of love, the deliverance from death.

True eternity, therefore, is neither the rejection of time nor the transcendence of time. It is fellowship with a real other whose presence is the overcoming of the past and our possibility of a future. As such, eternity is a reality experienceable in this world.

The mode of the experience of eternity is love, and love is time in the dimension of the future. Therefore, the essential characteristic of love is the attitude of waiting. Eternity is the fellowship between the present, which is the life of the self, and the future (*shōrai*), which is the presence of the other. The perfect unity of future and present, or the perfect presence of the future is eternity. Where this unity comes about, there is no room for a past, and no room for a future as simply something that has "not yet come" (*mirai*). This is an important insight in Hatano's understanding of time. An understanding of the presence of God as our future (*shōrai*) is as much a judgment upon a life oriented to a merely spatially defined future (*mirai*) as it is upon a life oriented to the past. Both are a form of death. As he says, it is foolish to talk about what has "not yet come" (*mirai*) while actually experiencing eternity.[23]

The life of love as *agapē* is also a judgment upon life as self-realization. For the relation of *agapē* is initiated in the will to let others be. A fellowship of this sort is impossible for the strategy of self-realization, where others become the mediators of a man's own sense of selfhood. *Agapē* overcomes all mediating principles. *Agapē* attempts to derive its principle unconditionally from others.[24] Drawing upon Swedish Bishop Anders Nygren's conclusions about *agapē* Hatano acknowledges Augustine's use of *agapē* but criticizes Augustine because he did not keep love unconditioned. He allowed an element of self-realization to enter.[25]

Religion occurs when a living person encounters an absolute reality. What transpires in this meeting is, from God's side, revelation; from man's side, experience.[26] Religion thus answers the problem of natural and cultural life which is the problem of how to find an other who can save us from the drift into nothingness. What is left when everything turns to nothingness? A fellowship of life is left between creator and creature. That is what is revealed in religion. To look persistently to relations with others for deliverance from the nothingness of life is futile because these others are immersed as we are in nature and infected as we are with culture. Our problem is how to find a real other not thus caught up in the human predicament. The revelation of that other is the turning point to religion.

Only an other who has the qualities associated with a holy creator is sufficiently absolute, sufficiently free from potentiality, sufficiently real, to supply the conditions for a fellowship of life that is *agapē*. As holy creator, God is the true other, the truly real, the source of love, the hope of eternity. To say that God is holy is to say that he maintains his reality under all circumstances as an other. As holy, God is the one reality impenetrable by the human effort at self-realization.

The experience of the holy reality of God is an experience of obedience. It is comparable to the experience of a baby at the breast of its mother. In the life of culture the self attempts to annex every other self just as a baby feeds off its mother. There comes a moment in the experience where the assertiveness of the self comes up against the irreducible reality of the other. At that moment obedience must supplant self-assertion. In religion, the holy reality of God as other is experienced by the self as fear and trembling, just as a child for the first time becomes aware of the independent otherness and authority of his mother.[27] It is because the real God encounters man with such abruptness and authority that Hatano gives so central a place to the characterization of God as a " God of power." [28]

How can anything resembling a fellowship of love occur with a reality that maintains itself in such holy otherness? The answer is that to have an experience of the holiness of God one must have an immediate encounter with God. For " if there is any religion which preaches the existence of a mediator between the absolute other and the human subject, either this mediator is not a third person but God himself [as in Christianity?], or the God is not actually a God and his holiness is not real holiness." [29]

But an experience of the presence of a holy God would mean no less than the annihilation of the self. The problem posed by such an encounter is how the self, " reduced to ashes in the fire of holiness," can ever regain its own reality and selfhood.[30] The answer to that is that the holy God is also the Creator. An absolute that lives simply in itself, remaining in its self-identity, will come to nothing in the end, just as the center of a circle when expanded into infinity will cease being a center and disappear into nothingness (as in the Buddhist concept of God?).[31] The doctrine of Creation is the religious answer to the need of a holy being for something outside itself, and creation *ex nihilo* is a fit symbol. For the self who understands himself as annihilated in the presence of the holiness of God also understands himself as brought out of this nothingness by God's creative act. The doctrine of creation *ex nihilo* instructs the self in the realization that the very acts by which God reduces man to nothing are the acts in which he confers wholeness of being upon man. Fellowship with God is a relation in which the nothingness implicit in that relation is also overcome. In the act of creation, being and nothingness come into existence at the same time. Creation is reducing others to nothingness in order to give them an imperishable existence. This is the fundamental difference between religious life and natural life. In natural life being is felt to precede nothingness. In religious life, oriented as it is to the love act of the Holy Creator, nothingness precedes being. God creates out of nothing. Man holds his being as a nothing before God's holiness. The being man has is the being God confers by his holy presence, which is *agapē*.

Erōs is an infinite love, a love of everything, a vampire's thirst that attempts to draw everything into the orbit of self-realization. Characterizing culture as it does, *erōs* is a fundamentally man-centered, anthropological concern. Does a theology of *agapē*, then, escape the charge of anthropocentrism? Ludwig Feuerbach and Martin Buber are important in Hatano's answer to that question. Feuerbach is important because he believed that man exists in acknowledgment of some other self, a " thou." This social category took Feuerbach's position beyond idealistic anthropologies built on intellection and *self*-realization.[32] Buber is important to Hatano by virtue of what seems to be his understanding that individuality is conferred upon one by the presence of a " thou," as a partner in life.[33]

In Japan, just as in the theological world in general, the understanding of Martin Buber's book *I and Thou* has been overtaken by Gogarten's somewhat different use of the personal category, particularly in his volume *I Believe in the Triune God*.[34] " I-Thou " for Buber is a kind of reality, distinctly different from another kind of reality called " I-it." That is, for Buber the reality is neither I nor Thou, neither I nor it, but I-Thou and I-it. For Gogarten, as for Hatano, the hyphen loses its cruciality and thus the references to I and Thou have a changed connotation. For them, I without Thou is not history, for history is a community concept. I without Thou is reality in solitude; and I with Thou is reality in love. The emphasis in Hatano, as in Gogarten, is on what is called "personalistic realism," where the person is regarded as independently real, but only in the presence of an other person. For Buber, however, I-it can as easily characterize one's relation to a person as to a thing; and I-Thou includes one's relation to the things of nature, and is not restricted to personal relations.

Buber's book first appeared in Japanese in 1958, thirty-five years after its appearance in German. Gogarten's book, however, appeared in Japanese a matter of months after its appearance in German. It is even more significant that the title given to Buber's *I and Thou* in the Japanese translation is *Solitude and Love.* I take this as evidence of Gogarten's victory over Buber in the I-Thou field. There may be some Oriental reasons for this susceptibility to Gogarten. In Shinto thinking, for instance, the concept of the ego by itself has no social meaning. The "I" is necessarily the "private one." Hence, to save the social dimension for the ego, the Japanese would have to set another ego over against it, as Hatano and Gogarten do. For Buber, the ego is intrinsically social, that is, a reality in the dimension of I-Thou. On the other hand, "Thou" in Japanese is a word used by a superior when he addresses his inferior, as by the emperor to his subjects. Hence one could scarcely expect Japanese theologians and philosophers to employ it joyfully at a moment in national history when democratic categories are replacing feudal categories. I must confess, however, notwithstanding these conjectures, that according to the publisher, the Japanese title for Buber's book was simply an invention contrived to sell the book to a people for whom solitude and love have a great deal of appeal.

For Hatano, then, the corollary of God's holy creativity in the fellowship of love is the complete and unconditional abandonment of the self. The role of man in the fellowship with God is characterized by sacrifice, devotion, unselfishness. The most descriptive terms for this relation Hatano draws from the vocabulary of Buddhism. The life of *agapē* is a *kyochi* life, " an I going away," or a life of *botsuga*, " a self sinking down or undermining itself." The method of self-abandonment can be illustrated from ordinary experience, such as the experience of rigorously eliminating certain forms of luxury and pleasure from one's life in order to accumulate money for the fulfillment of noble aims. Hatano could well have had in mind instances of Japanese students who regularly fast in order to buy a book.

Unconditional self-abandonment in the presence of God is what is meant by the life of faith. Faith is obedience, thanks, and trust. Faith is any act of human response to the love of God that is also regarded as an act of God toward man.[35] Faith is the double movement of prayer and ethics, the act of participating in eternity while standing in time, grasping the hand of the other while emptying one's own self.[36]

As prayer, faith is gratitude for grace, the confession of man's own nothingness. Prayer is the word of man, yet it is a word offered to a real other, an absolute reality. Within the understanding of God as a real, independent other, prayer is given its true place for the first time. The prayer is not looked upon as a preface of incantation to an act of magic. Prayer is viewed as the response of self-surrender to the initiative of a holy creator. In the Meiji era the Emperor of Japan once told his people that if they lived right God would protect them, even if they did not pray. That may well be the background for Hatano's epic statement about prayer. " Man prays to God," he said, " because God saves man without his prayers." [37]

As ethics, faith is a movement of love toward one's fellow man. The extent of the value of another person has nothing to do with *agapē*.[38] For *agapē* requires the complete and unconditioned abandonment of the self toward others. *Agapē* is fulfilled not simply in great heroic deeds but in the trifling, ordinary circumstances of everyday life. In every human relation *agapē* sees a real person in the individual who is with him. *Agapē* lets this person be an end in himself and not a means. Others are always allowed to be other and never simply an element in a man's own program of self-realization. A self that lives in the time of *agapē* begins all relations with others by abandoning his own egocentricity. He deliberately strives to live in and from the standpoint of others.[39] It is the very content of eternal life that the I and the Thou shall remain together with God, rejoicing in God and giving thanks.

The distinction between an ethics of *agapē* and an ethics of *erōs* is clear. In *erōs* the end of man's behavior is self-assertion toward others. *Agapē* interrupts all acts of self-assertiveness by the presence of the impenetrable dignity of the holy. *Erōs* directs itself to values that become the object of self-realization. *Agapē* aims at communion or fellowship with another being. " Faith works as love toward man." [40] Love surrenders itself to another person as to a God-given reality, hence always proceeds on the basis of the concrete reality of another. A typical example of such love is love toward an enemy. A man gives himself to the enemy with the personal concern with which a mother gives herself to a child, with *itsukushimi*, that is, mercy, devotion, service, in short, *agapē*. Through this form of action, man lives in the imperishable world of eternity while still existing in the time of others.[41]

"Love always communicates in symbols."[42] A symbol is the only vehicle of communication by which God can address man without annihilating man's selfhood irrevocably, and it is the only vehicle by which one man may communicate with another in such a way as to let the other be. Therefore, symbolization occurs only at the religious level. In natural and cultural life the content of life is the object of symbolization, but the act of communication that transpires there is called "expression," in deliberate contrast with symbol. For expression is communication in the interest of self-realization. Expression communicates content, but symbol makes the very *center* of life the object of communication. Symbol communicates in such a way as to let the reality be what it is in the act of referring to the reality. Symbol, therefore, is the principle that makes communication with a real other possible. A meeting between two personal realities is a relation between their very centers. Hence, symbolism and reality are co-ordinate concepts.

The experience of human limitedness is an instance of what Hatano means by a symbol. The theological correlate to which it points is the doctrine of Creation. The experience of living as a newly given self or the experience of the recreation of one's annihilated self in an act of boundless grace is also a symbol. The theological correlate is in the doctrine of salvation.[43]

The symbol, that is, must not be asked to reveal an intellectual content. It is expected to expose the center of a reality. In that sense the symbol is an instrument of revelation. By it, something hidden can be revealed. In the broad sense, all symbol is revelation. In the narrower sense, revelation is symbolic in respect of being a fellowship between the divine reality and the self. That fellowship is a thoroughgoing symbolization. Something hidden becomes thereby revealed; something transcendent becomes immanent. When the symbol is reduced to an intellectual content, it becomes something else, which Hatano calls allegory. The symbol is coincidental with eternity; the allegory is not. The allegory, however, intends or means that coincidence. In that respect, allegory, to which we are limited in all theoretical expressions of the content of the faith, is not uncongenial to faith, even though inadequately expressive of it.[44]

The Christian experience of resurrection is one of Hatano's most vivid illustrations of the place of symbol. In Buddhism and in Western philosophies of immortality, life after death is understood at a purely cultural level. There, life after death is regarded as a continuation of this life, a condition of interminable successiveness, hence viewed as something painful, in the nature of punishment. The Christian doctrine of life after death, by contrast, is a doctrine of resurrection. In resurrection, man regains a life that has been lost. He comes into being from nothingness. Death for a Christian does not mean a shifting from one mode of being to another but the very destruction of life, the drifting of being into nonbeing. "All the thinkers of Christianity have been trying to evade this notion of death as the complete destruction of life. Where they succeed, the notion of resurrection means next to nothing."[45]

The resurrection of the dead is not a matter of sheer physiology or psychology, however, but of person. The person is only a problem for us in fellowship, and fellowship is achieved only through symbol. The body is pertinent to the understanding of resurrection, therefore, as the theater or passageway through which fellowship is accomplished by symbol. The life after death will have at its core, then as now, the love of man toward God and his fellow man. What is already seen in this world, but only in part, will be fully seen in the world to come. " The blind resistance of nature in this world will be changed into the dignity and glory of God. The arts and sciences of this world will perish, but the word of God will fill our ears and eyes in eternity. In this present world, ideas have authority in proportion to the excellence of cultural life. But in the next world where love is the unique, eternal reality, the concrete individual who was despised in this world may be the first to be resurrected by God's power." [46]

The work of Hatano represents the highest level of intellectual maturity in Japanese theology today. The reason which prompts that conclusion would also lead one to conclude that the expression of Christianity which prevails in the Non-Church movement is a relatively immature expression. Non-Church Christianity in its adherence to the Bible alone is puristic, reminiscent of children who never venture beyond their own yards. Hatano's position, aside from the question of its acceptability in details, is Christianity in adult dialogue with the world. More than the monologue of evangelism, it is the dialogue of a Christianity secure enough in its own right to know it can listen to and profit from the insights of alien faiths and philosophies without surrendering to them.

The Non-Church movement anchors Japanese Christianity to its unique source in the Bible. Watanabe, requiring Japanese Christianity to reflect upon its method of appropriating its source, gives more credence to the role of the church in interpretation than Non-Churchism does. Kumano builds a systematic theology upon the whole tradition of the church, not simply upon the Bible, nevertheless giving the apostolic tradition of the Bible a normative power that is not inherent in subsequent church tradition. Kitamori finds one theme in Christianity by which everything in faith and practice is illuminated. Where Non-Churchism adduces the source of the Christian faith, and Kumano elucidates that source into a system, Kitamori in his discernment of " the pain of God " provides the system with a soul.

Hatano, without bypassing these preparatory stages, more fully manifests the courage to be as a Christian than is evident in these others. In his system, the members of the household of faith can feel the door of the church open upon the world. There is, of course, no intention of calling for a vote to determine which of these positions excels. No one of them could be replaced by an other. Each has its function in the development of theology in Japan today. I am only observing that in a land in which Protestant Christianity is a mere child and the church a minority group, it is impressive to find so muscular an evidence of Christian maturity as Hatano has provided in " the theology of the time of love."

V | *The Maturity of Japanese Theology*

THE PURPOSE OF THIS VOLUME HAS BEEN TO CHARACTERIZE Japanese theology today. I have chosen to do so by way of the positions of several outstanding scholars and of a dominant Christian movement, the Non-Church group. Such a method has the virtue of doing for the relatively unknown Japanese situation what analysts usually do when they deal with more influential areas of Christendom. The maturity of a Christian people is often evidenced in whether it is producing a theological genre of its own. The appearance of commanding points of view in Japan can be taken as a sign that such a genre is developing there.

An even more reliable sign of Christian maturity can be found in the way in which the theologians of the church conceive the issues of the faith at any given time, the extent to which they enter into dialogue with other theologians occupied with these same issues, and the clarity and cogency of their resolution of these issues. A view of Japanese theology would be incomplete, therefore, without a sketch of just how some of the major theological issues of the time are being handled in Japan. To deal with that in a concluding chapter should have several distinct advantages. First, it is an opportunity to detail some of the insights of theologians who have not been singled out thus far for extensive treatment, but who are nonetheless in the front ranks of theological activity in Japan. Second, it is an occasion for expanding upon the contributions of the major theologians dealt with, whose views up to now in this discussion have been deliberately confined to the range of their unique contribution. Third, it is a final chance to place Japanese theological reflection in the context of more universal theological concerns and thus further to illustrate the plausibility and the importance of taking Japanese Christendom seriously as a dialogical partner in the world church.

1. *The Role of Philosophy in Theology.* Japanese theology has come to flower in the period of Christendom whose theologians will someday be known as the "post-*Nein!* fathers." In 1934, Karl Barth spoke his loud "No!" against all efforts to perpetuate natural theology as a legitimate theological operation. Ever since, theology has been forced to consider, more carefully than probably at any other time in the history of the church, precisely what status should be given to claims to truth that appear outside the special revelation of God in Jesus Christ. The discipline that is most often under suspicion among theologians is philosophy, because no other "natural," nontheological source has been so eagerly employed in theological formulation.

Is any knowledge of God available to man in such an extrarevelational discipline as philosophy? Is there a natural revelation that is not dependent upon the special revelation of God in Christ? If not, what can be said to be the theological usefulness of the discipline?

One of the views widely characteristic of Japanese theology is expressed by the New Testament scholar Prof. Jisaburō Matsuki. In his discussion of the one Biblical text usually adduced in support of natural theology, Rom. 1:20, he asserts that it is wrong to ask if there is " natural revelation " in Paul. Paul nowhere consciously discusses it. Why not? Because Paul understands that " God has *now* decided to save the people through ' the foolishness of preaching.' " According to Matsuki, " knowledge of God " has two connotations in Paul's understanding. First, it means to be known by God. Second, it means to adore God – to fear, obey, love, and glorify him. The " natural " knowledge of God breaks with both these forms of knowledge. When a man says at the height of his piety or his philosophy that he " knows God," he " expresses the supreme sin," which is disobedience. For in the first place, he has not known God as God has chosen to reveal himself, that is, in the foolishness of preaching. Through that knowledge man understands he *is known* by God. In the second place, his knowledge of God has not been synonymous with adoration and obedience.[1]

Yoshitaka Kumano has made a similar analysis, although in a more conciliatory tone. Philosophical knowledge of God is not ruled out because it is impossible, but simply because it is not the intended object of faith. The object of faith is the personal knowledge mediated historically in Jesus Christ. The knowledge of faith is not an immediate intuition of God or a knowledge mediated by nature or history in general. It should be noticed, however, that faith does not proceed in the absence of knowledge. Faith is itself the knowledge with which Christianity is bound up. Hence, knowledge is not something added to faith. It is faith. Faith is nothing but knowing God as he has made himself known, and that is necessarily a reasoning activity.

But given the particular conditions under which the knowledge of faith arises, based as it is in historical revelation, the knowledge of faith produces a different kind of intellectual activity from the knowledge of philosophy.[2] One ought not to conclude from that difference, however, that theology competes with philosophy. It simply deepens our philosophical, that is, our natural understanding.[3]

These attitudes toward philosophy expressed by Matsuki and Kumano seem to prevail in Japanese theology. Considering that fact, a Christian who takes philosophy seriously does so at some peril to his reputation as a theologian. For it is difficult to tell when a man is using philosophy as a second source of Christian knowledge alongside God's revelation in Christ or simply as a means of expressing the profundity of Christian truth at an urbane level. One of the theologians who persists in taking this philosophical risk is Takenosuke Miyamoto. In the introduction to his *Philosophy as Symbol*[4] he explicitly states that his work is " not directly bound up with Christian faith. It is mere philosophy." Yet he does regard it as " the concrete cultural expression of a Christian." The position is strongly reminiscent of his teacher Hatano.

According to Miyamoto, the difference between a religion and a philosophy is a difference in starting point. A religion is established through faith in divine revelation. The " science " based on this revealed faith is theology. What, then, is philosophy? Philosophy is " the general logical self-consciousness of that which symbolizes the transcendent." As such, it does not serve the divine revelation directly. The witness to revelation stands on faith. Philosophy – at least, " philosophy as symbol " – stands on love that is grounded in faith, but it does not stand on revelation. For this reason, philosophy and theology must be distinguished but they ought not to be separated. For even the revelation needs to be expressed symbolically, which it is the special strength of philosophy to accomplish. A philosophy of symbol, therefore, can clearly elucidate what a natural theology generally wants to know, yet without at the same time falling into natural theology. It can keep alive the concrete cultural symbols that point to the transcendent one, but only religion can *name* the transcendent. Nevertheless, philosophy can provide a vehicle for the concrete cultural expression of the revelation of God to which the Christian religion witnesses.[5] In his later volume, Miyamoto devotes himself to philosophy more clearly conceived as a valid operation within theology. He calls it a theological philosophy of religion, or apologetics as a department of theology.[6]

The theologian most responsible for self-consciousness in Japan over the place of philosophy in theology is Enkichi Kan, professor at St. Paul's, an Anglican university in Tokyo. In 1953, he made a study of "the problem of philosophy of religion in theology," which he called *Reason and Revelation.*[7] For Kan it was a decisive study because prior to the war he had worked in the liberal Protestant tradition in which the distinction between philosophy and theology was not particularly called for. However, following the war he was taken up into the dialectical theology movement and in this particular volume he provides the grounds for his decision between dialectical theology and the more philosophical theology of the late nineteenth-century Continental liberals, Troeltsch, Herrmann, and Wobbermin. These theologians, he believes, developed a rational philosophy of religion in which revelation is grounded in the reason.

The dialectical theology, represented in Kan's work

principally by Karl Barth and Emil Brunner, regarded philosophy of religion in the older, liberal sense as a ghost compared with dogmatic theology. Kan is prepared in this study to applaud the opinion that, since the development of dialectical theology, the ghost has vanished.[8] But he is ready to rematerialize the ghost for one purpose only, and that purpose is exclusively theological. Some discipline must preside over the decision as to where the line should be drawn between the operations of revelation and the operations of reason. That is the problem of determining the foundation of theology as "learning." "The task of philosophy of religion in theology," he writes, "is learning, which deals with the relation between religion and philosophy. This relation can be described as the relation between reason and revelation or between learning and theology." [9] There are two ways of doing this. One is the old, liberal style where revelation is grounded in reason, the other is a new dialectical style where reason is grounded in revelation. Only the latter can be regarded as a properly "theological philosophy of religion." Kan considers Emil Brunner the clearest example of this type.[10] In this definition, theology shows how revelation, which cannot be reached by reason, nevertheless clarifies the ambiguity and distortion of reason and finally satisfies reason's quest for truth by revealing the unknown God to it.

Theologians now widely presume that Karl Barth annihilated Brunner's position in his tract called *Nein!*, charging Brunner with natural theology. Kan's distinction between Barth and Brunner, however, is very cautious. While Brunner is logically right, he says, Barth is practically right,[11] and "of course, I start from Barth." [12] Kan's practical rejection of Brunner's method is based upon his belief that Brunner's philosophy of religion tries to augment man, building upon something in man – such as his unconscious rational yearning to know God – whereas Barth's "philosophy of religion" witnesses to God. Brunner perfects man; Barth turns man to God, remaking him. For Brunner, the fight between revelation and reason occurs only at the entrance to the church; for Barth it occurs inside the church. That means that for Brunner the philosophical problem of theology is how to make a point of contact for the revelation in the reason. For Barth, only God can deal with that problem.[13]

As has been pointed out in the previous chapter, Kan repudiates Hatano's philosophy of religion as an illustration of the old liberal method, which placed the understanding of the revelation upon the foundation of the reason. In so doing, Hatano is said to have awarded philosophy of religion a higher rank than theology itself.[14] My judgment, based on Hatano's works called *Philosophy of Religion* and *Time and Eternity*, was that Kan is wrong about Hatano. Hatano's later works deserve to be placed within the frame of reference that Kan calls "theological philosophy of religion." There are two reasons why that is so. First, they explicitly presuppose the authority of the Christian revelation, as do Miyamoto's works. Second, the Christian religion is shown to be a personalistic manifestation of eternity, which goes beyond philosophy as *agapē* goes beyond *erōs*. Kan, however, misses one important element in Hatano's philosophy of religion, and thus in Miyamoto's. That is the point at which it breaks out of the mold that limits philosophy of religion to the problem of reason and revelation. For Hatano, theology demands a philosophy. That is, the view of life implicit in the Christian revelation must articulate itself into a philosophical view. Any theological relation to philosophy that does not go that far cannot be thought to have taken philosophy seriously enough. On that basis, Hatano, who rejects both Barth and Brunner as philosophically inadequate, interestingly finds Barth more palatable than Brunner. He can "forgive" Barth because Barth only "dismisses" philosophy. But he must reject Brunner because Brunner has only a utilitarian approach to philosophy. Brunner "uses" philosophy, thus shows he has no true "love" for philosophy.[15]

A younger Christian philosopher, Kazuo Mutō of Kyoto University, breaks out of Kan's classification in another direction. Philosophy to him is not simply related to Christian faith as its symbolic expression. It is as well a negative moment in theology itself. For that reason, Mutō believes that Kierkegaard and not Barth is the best representative of Kan's classification, "theological philosophy of religion." For in Kierkegaard, philosophy does not overcome theology and theology does not overcome philosophy. A dialectical relation is sustained. In Barth, however, theology cuts itself off from philosophy completely and therefore takes over the role of philosophy, as Scholasticism did in the Middle Ages. In Kierkegaard, philosophy retains its autonomy. Yet, by virtue of its existential depth, it contains in itself a negative moment against theology, an apologetic moment that dares to pose the question of Christianity's adequacy to answer the fundamental predicament of human existence. A philosophy of this sort, embraced by theology, cannot be absorbed by theology; but it can serve to keep theology relevant to the cultural situation by preventing its becoming self-enclosed.[16]

The issue that dominated Continental theology in the thirties and that was believed to have been settled by Barth is still being kept open in Japanese theology. Philosophy is not considered to be a source for the knowledge of God alongside the revelation. To that extent the Japanese are with Barth. Whether that decision reduces philosophy to a mere instrument of dogma is the question that remains. Hatano's work suggests a basis for allowing philosophy to have an integrity of its own. On his basis the existence of a religious revelation need not imply the irrelevance of philosophy. The content of the revelation can provide philosophy with a source of understanding not intrinsically available to philosophy and on the basis of which philosophy itself, which otherwise only poses the religious question, becomes philosophy of religion, deliberately addressing itself to the broad issues of natural and cultural life. Mutō has suggested, moreover, how philosophy can be taken more intimately into theology – without being absorbed by it – as its negative, self-critical moment, and as an occasion for its sensitivity toward, and communion with, culture in general.

2. *The Communication of Christianity to Culture.* Tokutarō Takakura, one of the few outstanding forerunners of contemporary Japanese theology, once listed what he believed to be the two main problems for modern Christianity in Japan. The first was to rediscover the meaning of Christianity. As I have shown, the Japanese theologians are unanimous in their seriousness over that concern. The second problem that Takakura cited was the task of finding a relation between Christianity and culture.[17] After one hundred years of Protestant Christianity in Japan it is important that the theologians have a lively memory concerning how the faith first broke into their culture. The fact, for instance, that the first Protestant congregation was composed of two Buddhist priests, one physician, and five samurai seems to lend historical credence to the value of a strategy for relating Christian faith to culture. There are,

of course, exceptions in the memory of the church that abate one's enthusiasm for strategies. It ought never to be forgotten, for instance, that Uchimura once gave his non-Christian father a four-volume commentary on the Gospel of Mark. It was written by a German missionary, in the Chinese language. Yet it converted his father to Christianity.

What are the characteristics in Japanese culture today that pose obstacles to receiving the Christian faith? My answer to this question is of a rather random sort, based not at all upon observations I have made, but only upon statements by Japanese theologians themselves. They range from the very obvious problems that could prevail anywhere to the more subtle problems closer to the Japanese situation.

Materialism is often cited as a barrier to Christian faith. Evidently the preoccupation with things, or with security in the world, is as passionate for those who do not have much as for those who have. For the Japanese are an ascetic people in comparison with Western nations. The barrier to the spirit must lie in the direction of the passion and not in the degree of one's acquisitions.

Nationalism has recurrently been in open contest with Christianity. Existing quietly at the level of wounded pride or nursed hopes makes nationalism no less a threat, spiritually. Pride in the appropriation of Western ways since the war has balanced nationalism in a most curious way. Shall one again become a Christian in Japan because it is now popular there to face the West? Or does facing the West and adopting its ways become a surrogate faith, making Christianity superfluous? Either is a possibility in the present, and either in its own way is a block to authentic faith.

Feudalism, particularly manifested in the home, is rapidly being overcome in larger urban communities, but it persists in the rural areas. For the stability of Japanese society in this transitional era, residual feudalism may be an important fact. To the church, whose evangelism is extending more and more to rural areas, feudalism is an almost impenetrable wall. In a feudalistically structured Japanese family a decision to become a Christian is not a private decision. It radically affects the entire group. That fact virtually forces tender converts to become social martyrs in their first Christian step. Feudalism in the social structure, which expresses itself as paternalism, is a less obvious but probably more profound block to effective Christian evangelism. Christianity cannot work within it without seeming to endorse it. Hence, the Christian faith becomes associated with a system of things where employers smile beneficently upon employees but where the question of the independent rights of employees is rarely allowed to come up.[18]

Other faiths, especially the old and more indigenized faiths, would seem to be the most obvious and natural barrier to Christianity. Yet non-Christian faiths are taken very lightly by Japanese Christians.[19] Of course, no Japanese will say what Westerners are fond of observing, namely, that the Japanese live in a spiritual vacuum. Shinto shrines and Buddhist temples have a hold on the people, even after that hold may have lost its rationale. However, the syncretistic way in which the people relate to these faiths may be a sign of the lack of seriousness of these faiths as religions. For instance, it is not at all unusual for the same family to celebrate its weddings at the shrine and its funerals at the temple. In comparison with these venerable faiths, a number of new religions have sprung up since the war and their phenomenal numerical success and evident gratification of the needs of the people are a sharp rebuke to Christians, especially to a church whose growth in the same period is almost negligible.

The discussion of the Non-Church movement in Chapter I pointed up the curious fact that Christianity can be its own worst enemy. When it develops a form of ecclesiasticism largely imitative of the West, it is courting *ecclesiastical colonialism.* That is a block to Christian advance in Japan of which the churches themselves are quite aware. In 1951, when fifty-three former Presbyterian Churches in the United Church of Christ in Japan (*Kyōdan*) withdrew to form " the Japan Christ Church," colonialism in finance and policy was the main reason given (although a " narrow Calvinism " in theology also gave the group some homogeneity). The churches that remain together in the *Kyōdan*, however, do not deceive themselves about their weaknesses as a church. In a recent statement of a program of evangelism for the *Kyōdan*, certain factors in the church's life were confessed as hindrances to evangelism. These included a lack of vital contact with life, pastor-centeredness of the churches sometimes called " ministerial anarchy," a Western theological ideology unrelated to the Japanese masses, and the virtual engulfment of the church by its non-Christian environment.

Nihilism in the Orient is a block to the coming faith in a sense that may not be true of nihilism in the West. Nihilism is the general spirit in a culture that despairs of any meaning at all. In Western culture, existential philosophy has been chiefly an articulation of such threats of meaninglessness. But, existential philosophy has kept alive the ambiguity in nihilism. Existentialists can choose meaning in the face of the possible meaninglessness of life. Faith is as plausible as despair. In this sense, Prof. Yasumasa Ōshima's enormous volume on the tragic element in Western thought is a profoundly Western book, for the tragic element in existence, expressed in contemporary literature as existentialism, has led Oshima to the very threshold of faith in Jesus Christ.[20]

There are more typical Oriental responses to nihilism than acts of faith, however. One of these is suicide. Nevertheless, the Japanese detect a difference between present-day acts of suicide and the traditional *harakiri*. Traditionally, suicide was unrelated to nihilism, for it was an act of taking one's life in the interest of some high meaning, such as loyalty to a feudal lord or compensation for an act of dishonor. Today, even suicide in Japan has become Westernized. One may now take his life out of a sense of the meaninglessness and unreasonableness of existence, or simply out of boredom, as suicides have usually done in the West.

The other response to nihilism is of a religious or philosophical sort. The distinctive Oriental method of facing nothingness is to sink more deeply into it rather than leaping out of or beyond it. The reasons for that are philosophically subtle and could be found in the philosophy of Kitarō Nishida. The effect upon life, whatever the philosophical reasoning behind it, is an alternative to Christian solutions at several significant points. The process of " sinking into nothing " is unhistorical, unsocial, and acosmic. That is, to meet nihilism in the Oriental way is to depreciate life in the world and to isolate oneself from human community.[21]

One of my interpreters was once asked what quality he believed to be most important in a missionary to Japan. His immediate reply was that a missionary must have the capacity to understand nihilism. Note that he did not suggest nihilism as something to be exploited, as vendors of drinks exploit victims of drought. Oriental nihilism solves itself from within itself. Years ago, the historian Froude, in a lecture on "The Science of History," observed quite sanely, "We remember Japan, the spot in all the world where earthquakes are most frequent, and where at the same time there is the most serene disbelief in any supernatural agency whatsoever." Japanese nihilism does not bring its devotees to their knees before religious solutions. That is why nihilism can be regarded as a block rather than a schoolmaster to faith.

One of the most plausible and profound analyses of cultural resistance to Christianity in Japan has been provided in the writings of Kazoh Kitamori. In his belief, the main hindrance to Christianity is the spirit of *aesthetic detachment* so characteristic of Japanese culture and expressed in its very aseptic poetic form called *haiku. Haiku* is a seventeen-syllable poetic form inaugurated by the seventeenth-century Zen Buddhist monk Bashō. The characteristic of the poetry, aside from the syllabic count, is its strangely noncommittal character, its objective detachment, the "pathos of things" in it. I cite one of Bashō's widely known poems:

> A branch shorn of leaves,
> A crow perching on it –
> This autumn eve.

The detached spirit in *haiku* has been so closely identified with what is most highly valued in Japan that every evidence of involvement, commitment, and the "pathos of persons" is looked down upon as unintelligent, rude, and uncouth. All people are divisible into two types, then: the *iki* or sophisticated and the *yabo* or uncouth. A Christian, who by the very nature of his faith surrenders himself to God through discipleship to Christ, is obviously *yabo*, the very characteristic most distasteful to the Japanese spirit. Hence, "*iki* people will have nothing to do with Christianity because of its *yabo*-ness." [22]

One ought not regard this barrier as universal, however, for there is also present in Japanese life what is called *bushidō*, or the warrior's code of readiness to be faithful unto death. This characteristic is manifested in the relation of a servant to his lord, in the samurai's devotion to battle, or in the *kami-kaze* tactics of the last war. Therefore, Kitamori's suggestive analysis of the aesthetic spirit in Japan at first glance seems counterbalanced by the understanding of a trait that makes it equally plausible for a Japanese to embrace a popular religion as if he were redeeming his master's honor in battle. Even Japanese children have a trait similar to *bushidō*, which appears in their relationships to other children. In some instances it is impossible for one child to have more than one friend, so all-consuming is the loyalty in the relation of friendship. The Japanese have even developed what they call a one-man dog, the *akita*. Emil Brunner was known to have regarded this ability for *exclusive attachment* as the chief barrier to Christianity in Japan. It is true that an absolute attachment to relative realities is a factor in the mechanisms of idolatry. It also seems true, however, that no samurai served two masters, and that a people who can develop a one-man dog should be able to worship only one God.

In his discussion of the Japanese penchant for detachment, however, Kitamori does not apparently mean to convey the impression that the *iki* trait is simple and tranquil. It may really be only one very tortured moment in a process designed to evade the seriousness of existence. In one of his writings he comments on the following lines of a contemporary poet Ishikawa.

> Even now in my eyes there is an impression of
> The dead face of my friend who was once very waggish.

Waggishness, or *hyōkin,* is what covers up the pale, tired look of the death mask. It also serves in this poem to indicate the whole spiritual situation of man. But, according to Kitamori, *hyōkin* exists in three different modes. The first mode is the situation in which a man is unconsciously waggish. He does not see the situation he is in. Living at the level of mere common sense, he is concerned only about his poses or how he appears. He is neither involved nor detached, but like a man riding in a crowded train who is satisfied to lose his existence by lapsing into anonymity for the duration of the trip. The second mode is the situation in which a man is self-consciously waggish. Here he deliberately attempts *not* to see the situation he is in. This seems descriptive of the moment that Kitamori has elsewhere explained by the *iki* temperament. Understood in this way, there is a kind of *bushidō* even in the *iki,* even in those who disdain *bushidō.* The very attitude of aesthetic detachment according to this analysis is a tension-filled commitment to overlook the seriousness of life. The third mode is called bashfulness. Here a man would yield to the temptation to enter into the situation of life with complete seriousness were it not for the presence of others observing him. This mode is the hardest to negotiate because of its comic character. It is the final exposé of the fact that sheer waggishness, the sheer camouflage of the seriousness of life, is no adequate way to cope with life.[23] Presumably the task of the poet and the theologian is to unmask the fraudulence of the *iki* way of life. That is, he must lead the waggish beyond the socially acceptable second mode to the existentially unacceptable third mode. From within that mode, he raises questions that border remarkably on the *yabo* or *bushidō* mentality. That characteristic will never be wholly foreign to a life of faith.

Considering these hindrances to Christian communication in Japan, how do the theologians estimate the role of apologetics, which is definable as the strategy of communicating Christianity to culture? Influenced as they are by dialectical theology and Barthianism one might expect the Japanese theologians to disavow apologetics. After all, in dialectical theology the purpose of Christianity is to put the world in crisis and not to build a bridge to it. In Karl Barth, " No " has been spoken as loudly to apologetics as to natural theology.

Paul Tillich and Reinhold Niebuhr have a hearing in Japan principally because of their apologetic concerns. As someone has observed, " Surrounded as it is by pagan culture, in Japan the issue between proclamation and apologetics is not raised." The truth of that claim seems verified by the fact that even the most thoroughgoing Barthians do not find Barth averse to apologetics. Barth has not said no to culture. It is simply that for him the way to say yes to culture is to look up to God.[24] Therefore, the Japanese are impressed that Karl Barth in his *Church Dogmatics* has evinced an interest in the Shinran sect of Buddhism and has revealed an understanding and appreciation equal to anything done in Japan. Kanō Yamamoto has even in his early, most Barthian writing proposed that modern Shinran Buddhism, which Francis Xavier once called a Lutheran heresy, " provides a window through which Christianity and Japan can meet." [25]

Again, in this connection Kitamori's thinking about communication seems most refreshing and balanced. Apologetics, he says, must avoid the tactic of *kyakubiki*, which can be translated into English as " the hard sell." Tourists who have never visited Japan might find it difficult to believe that high-pressure salesmanship is virtually nonexistent there. " Inviting one to be a customer almost by force evokes no attention " from the customer, as Kitamori says. Similarly, when a theology tries to force others to buy, it is a sign that the situation is lacking in power. " The hard sell " is rooted in techniques of apologetics. Authentic communication, however, must start from the power in the situation.[26] Theology has a right to become aggressive in its apologetic attacks upon culture only when rival solutions to the human predicament forget their relativity. These must be confronted and combated.[27] Unlike the Roman Catholic view of the relation of Christianity and culture, the Protestant view does not regard the movement from culture to faith as smooth and easy. There is no perfect analogy between nature and grace. That is why, for Kitamori, all properly evangelical apologetics will suffer a moment of pain in the contract with culture, the pain of the disjunction that is overcome only in faith.[28] To be in the church, invested by God with the gospel, however, is to shoulder that pain. The truth of the gospel is that God has taken full responsibility for man, who is other than God. The problem of communication is how to relate this gospel to a world that is other, alienated from God, and that lives by its unacceptance of God. The answer to that problem is in the responsibility of the church, which is the form the gospel takes in the world. The church assumes its responsibility for the world, however, only when believers are willing to assume some kind of concrete and effective solidarity with the world.[29]

3. *The Emergence of Ethics.* There is an impressive conviction among the Japanese theologians today that the point at which the Christian faith most closely touches Japanese culture is in the proclamation of the faith as ethics, when ethics is understood as the action of the church in its contribution to the arrival of a Christian culture.[30] In one of his published sermons, Zenda Watanabe has discussed the issue as to why the Christian church is so often referred to in Japan as " the place of hypocrites." It seems that during the days of the American military occupation of Japan following the war the behavior of the American soldiers did not always correspond with the ethical level expected of Christians. The direct criticism from the Japanese people was turned into an indirect compliment in Watanabe's sermon. As he said with unveiled irony, what the Japanese soldiers did in the South Seas was only cruel. But the American soldiers were hypocrites! Hypocrisy, however, exists only by virtue of a social standard of values in the light of which a man is compelled to appear better than he is. In American society there is a Christian way of thinking that is nonexistent in Japan. The moral standard in American culture is so high that even those who do not regard themselves as Christians are made to feel the authority of its morality, so great is Christianity's power there.[31]

The inference from this analysis would seem to be that the impact of Christianity upon Japan will be measurable in some sense in the effect that it has upon the ethical structure of Japanese life. Yet, it is popular for outsiders to observe that Japanese theology is eminently deficient in matters so practical as ethics. To what extent is that so? Judged by the contemporary views presented in this book, no theological position of a major sort today omits ethics as a salient emphasis. It has been seen, for instance, that the

Non-Church movement, notwithstanding its strategy of noninvolvement in Westernism, brought prophetic judgment upon the Imperial Government during the prewar years. This was due to its Biblical sense of transnational justice. Kumano based his ethics on predestination, eschatological history, or, what is the same, church existence. Ethics for him, therefore, was not simply the fulfillment of specific moral acts but the obedience of the whole person to a destiny under God. Ethics for him, then, involved not so much particular acts as it did an ultimate significance supporting these acts. Kitamori based his ethics upon an understanding of and participation in the pain of God. Again, for him, ethics was not the performance of particular human acts but the ability to understand the suffering of others as well as one's own suffering as symbols of the pain of God and then to act upon that understanding. The discernment of the pain of God in social problems makes it possible for the Christian realistically to cope with the source of the social problem, which is the sin, the occasion for God's pain. Finally, Hatano developed an ethic of concern for others that was based not upon the worthiness of the other but upon self-abandonment in the love of God. True community, which is the goal of ethics, is achievable only at the level of the religion of *agapē*.

Do not these summaries of Japanese theological ethics simply confirm the popular suspicion that Japanese theology is indifferent to ethics? How is it possible to deemphasize the specifiable moral act, as these views recurrently do, and still have ethics? The answer to that can be found in some of the unique sources underlying the ethics of Japanese theology.

One of these sources is dialectical theology. According to Kumano's account of dialectical theology, " all ethics have the same religious content and all religions have the same ethical content." What is unique in Christian ethics, then, alongside other religious and philosophical ethics? Other ethics do precisely what Christian ethics does in raising the question of the moral imperative. The difference is that in Christianity there is no presupposition, such as exists in general ethics, that the moral will has the power to execute its imperatives. The Christian ethic presupposes faith, and thus by exposing the corruption of the ethical nature in the human being brings all ethics under judgment. To ask the ethical question is to ask the question of human existence itself: Can one whose existence is destined to death attain any final good?

In a morality based upon faith, such as dialectical theology has developed, three positive results accrue. In the first place, legalism is transcended. The man of faith lives no longer under the curse of the question, What ought I do? because in God's gift of righteousness he has received the answer to the prior question, What am I? God's grace implies the indicative, not the imperative. In the second place, the ethics of faith is an ethic of love. Love and not law inspires the personal relations upon which the Christian ethic thrives. Because this love is personal, it will be expressed freely in every situation and not according to a pre-established program. In the third place, then, the Christian ethic is an ethic of freedom. This freedom is not immanent to one's being as man. It is an attribute of his relation to God. In the obedience to God in faith one is not called upon to carry out a moral program but to respond in readiness to God's orders.[32]

Another source of Japanese Christian ethics is the philosophical ethics of Tetsuo Watsuji. The concern of Watsuji is strikingly akin to the concern of the dialectical theology in respect of his definition of ethics as " the study of man." [33] In this very influential volume a large case is built upon the meaning of the words " ethics " and " man." The Japanese word for " ethics," *rinri*, is composed of two syllables. *Rin* means " a group " and *ri* means " reason." *Rinri*, or " ethics," therefore, is believed to concern both the community of men and the rational ground of that community.

The Japanese word for " man," *ningen*, literally means " between man and man." The supposition locked into this word is that man can be man only in relationship with others, that is, in community. The concept of ethics developed by Watsuji, therefore, is almost synonymous with philosophical anthropology or philosophy of culture, although avoiding what he believes to be the abstractness of that discipline. It is the task of ethics to place man in question. But the man in question can be properly addressed only at the level of his community with other men.[34]

A common source for Watsuji's ethics and the ethics of dialectical theology is traceable to the Danish theologian, Kierkegaard. The place of Kierkegaard in dialectical theology is patent. What is not so commonly known is that Watsuji, one of Japan's great non-Christian philosophers, was led to the study of ethics as he defined it by way of his study of Kierkegaard. As he says in the preface to his pioneering work on Kierkegaard, " The problem of Sören Kierkegaard is not that of rational philosophy. It had its source in the problem of the subjective existence, or how to live. Therefore, to look upon Kierkegaard's philosophy as basically ethical [as Watsuji did] was not wholly a mistake." [35]

Several factors of importance in this sophisticated ethical

position may not be readily apparent to Western Christendom. Mainly it is a Christian way between the equally unsatisfactory positions of pietism and social gospelism, which invaded Japan between the wars through the missionary enterprise. The social gospel position attempted to derive the ethics of the Kingdom of God from immanental value judgments, thus sponsoring as Christian ethics a combination of subjectivism and utilitarianism. Pietism, on the other hand, fostered an ethical climate in which, as one of Japan's sensitive novelists, Naoya Shiga, has said, Christians walk through the world like Japanese who hold a handkerchief to their mouths to keep sanitary: they seem to miss the common freedoms.

Again, it may come as a surprise in some quarters of the world that Japanese theologians draw inspiration for social ethics from Reinhold Niebuhr. " Niebuhr meets us where we are," Yamamoto asserts.[36] This Japanese theologian who several years earlier had called Karl Barth " the representative Christian of the Western world " [37] now finds that it is Reinhold Niebuhr who really penetrates such Asiatic problems as poverty.

The problem of implementing a social ethic in a society in which Christians have no balance of power is staggering. For that very reason, some theologians seem drawn to Hajime Tanabe's version of democratic socialism. In that view there seems to be a way of retaining the depth analysis of Kierkegaard's existentialism while at the same time tying up to the political power structure of socialism. " The socialization of existential philosophy " would overcome the dualism of existentialism's " isolated interiority " and Marxism's " environmental determinism." Without some such political elaboration of the Christian ethic, it will remain a " powerless ethic." [38] The logic of that alternative is that Christian ethics must always be church ethics. That is, the personal relation with Christ must be experienced as a relation with men in the concerted action of community.

Liberal Japanese Christianity, influenced by the social gospel at the turn of the century, is at least to be credited with an understanding of the sociopolitical dimension of the Christian ethic. All but one of the membership of the first official social democratic party in Japan were Christians. The platform of this group called for changes in the social structure: such as the abolition of the gap between the rich and the poor; a positive program of international peace spearheaded by the disbanding of the army and navy; public control and ownership of transportation, utilities, and natural resources; and the rights of labor to organize. The Japanese name most familiar to the West, which has yet to appear in this volume, is Toyohiko Kagawa. Kagawa's essential contribution to the Christian life of Japan is not theological but evangelistic and social. He will be remembered as one who understood the importance of expressing the Christian faith through the structures of society. That emphasis was the strength of the liberal Christianity of which Kagawa has been a leading representative. The weakness of the liberals was their tendency to *identify* Christianity with morals, thus weakening the significance of the doctrinal dimension.[39] The contemporary ethic of Japanese Christianity is not making that mistake.

On the other hand, the logic that Christian ethics should express itself through action in the community in general is not always so obvious in Japan. I think principally of the Non-Church theologians. Fujii, for instance, was content to speak to the population problem with piety rather than with political action, saying: "What is blessed is not to live on good land but to walk with God. In walking with

God even a desert is equal to a garden." [40] Is there not more prophetic courage than social wisdom in Yanaibara's pacifism when he says that " the way to spread the Christian gospel is not to conquer people but to die ourselves in order to let others live "? [41] For a professor of political philosophy, existing within the realistic power struggle of the Far East, this same Yanaibara seems a bit utopian when he suggests in deliberate antithesis to Marxists that " no matter how much you may change in the system, you cannot change the minds of the people." [42] That attitude gets traditional support in Non-Churchism, for it was typical of the founder, Uchimura. Uchimura had a profound social passion, unillumined by the dynamics of social change. He was satisfied that " society is no more than the collection of individuals " and that " social reform must start with the individual." [43] As he once put it in his cryptic way:

> A political problem is an economic problem. An economic problem is a moral problem. A moral problem is after all a religious problem. A political problem in the end is dependent on the faith of each individual.[44]

Current ethics among Japanese theologians, however, means something quite different from the more pietistic Non-Church emphasis, without at the same time simply repeating the social gospel. To say that political problems are basically religious problems is fundamentally acceptable. But one ought not to infer that individuals must be converted to the Christian religion before society can be affected positively by Christianity. Enkichi Kan once stated the position that still seems relevant. Salvation, he said, is a fundamentally ethical concept. It pertains not simply to the individual but to the society as well. In fact, " we believe there is no perfect salvation of the individual apart from the salvation of society." [45] Professor Matsuki has discerned this more politically aggressive role of Christians as far back as the apostle Paul. For Paul, he claims, "love in social affairs is not direct; it cannot bypass the state or the law, as Tolstoy did." [46]

If Watsuji's analysis of the Japanese "climate" is correct, the supposed lag in Japanese Christianity's assumption of social responsibility has one very plausible explanation. The Japanese are what he calls a *genkan* personality. The *genkan* is the elevated platform just inside the front door of the Japanese home at which one leaves his shoes when he enters. Along with his shoes he leaves the concerns of the outside world and lives only for his family. Watsuji regards this simple practice merely as a symbol of a national trait. The trait explains for Watsuji why a father who sees his neighbor's son in trouble can "pass by on the other side." Yet the same man would do anything for his own son. A woman who would bow to the floor in the presence of a visitor in her home would push her way ahead of another person in order to get a seat on a train. The *genkan* personality's responsibility to the world stops at his own front door. Fathom the spectacle, then, of a people with this characteristic suddenly being required to assume the responsibilities of democratic government. The Japanese Diet, elected to represent the people as a whole, is constituted of *genkan* personalities who have not understood responsibility beyond immediate family interests. So Watsuji charges. If that kind of indisposition to social responsibility is characteristic of the Japanese as a whole, it is understandable that Japanese Christians would find the social implementation of the Christian faith a somewhat puzzling responsibility.

Some might think that there are real grounds for pessimism about the ability of so numerically insignificant and so socially unpracticed a group as the Japanese Christians ever to influence high-level political and social policy in Japanese life. There are grounds for optimism, however, that the Christian theologians are sensitive to the profound dimensions of ethical responsibility, including man's obedience to God and his implementation of that obedience through the power structures of Japanese society. Christians know that a nation need not first become a church in order to reflect the judgment and the creative power of the Christian ethic.

4. *The Consciousness of History*. Christian ethics in Japanese theology is to be understood fundamentally as a theology of culture and a point of departure for significant action. A Christian self-consciousness, rooted in God's revelation to human history, will express itself as ethics. The ethics of the Christian faith is a revolutionary historical principle that inspires the very reformation of history.[47]

Probably the most up-to-date, most enlightened facet of Japanese theology is its analysis of the historical character of the Christian faith. This claim may be a bit startling, considering the long-standing belief that Oriental people take time and the world very lightly. For instance, it is only since the last war that the Japanese people have developed an uneasy conscience over their calendar system. The uneasy conscience is not over the fact that it does not adopt the Western system, which centers in the advent of Jesus. It is simply that the Japanese calendar has no base in history at all, but rests upon mythology.

The question whether the Japanese have shared the aversion to history said to be characteristic of the Orient in general may deserve a second look. Traditionally, China seems to have been preoccupied with nature, where nothing actually " happens " as it does in history. In Japan, Shinto has clearly perpetuated the same Oriental preoccupation with nature. Curiously, however, the center of Japanese art is not nature but man. The striking thing about Japanese art from the Fujiwara and Kamakura periods is the way the painted scrolls unfold like a moving picture of the history of man. It seems but a short step of the imagination from such a scroll to what theology today is calling *Heilsgeschichte*.[48]

Another way of expressing the popular assumption about the Orient is to say that a philosophy of history could not have developed there, for it has been dominated by Buddhism, a nonhistorical faith. Buddhism is a religion that desires to save the world without changing it. Christianity, on the other hand, while transcending the world, nevertheless realizes itself in and through the world. In Buddhism, the Dharma-buddha is superior to the incarnate Buddha. That is to say, the important matter for Buddhism is not the man Buddha but the truth he preserved. It would seem, therefore, that a land whose religious tradition has been formed by Buddhism would have no particular fondness for or understanding of what is involved in history.

Masatoshi Doi of Dōshisha University, to whom I am indebted for the foregoing comparison of Buddhism and Christianity, suggests quite a different conclusion. One exception to Buddhist indifference to history is found in a form of Buddhist eschatology called " end-Dharma," which developed in Japanese Buddhism. In the year A.D. 767 a Buddhist scholar named Dengyō divided history into three periods. The first period was comprised of five hundred years of right Dharma. The second part was characterized by one thousand years of devotion to images. The third part will last one hundred thousand years and is called the end-Dharma. The strategy of this philosophy of history resembles the Marxian dialectic and the Christian concept of "the right time," or *kairos*. That is, according to this Buddhist view of history, it would be historically irresponsible to perpetuate the laws and methods of one period into the time of another period. Each period has its own unique way of life.

In subsequent years the Genshi, Hōnen, Shinran, Jien, and Nichiren developments of Buddhism in Japan all emphasized some form of Dengyō's philosophy of history. It is even observed by Doi that in the Nichiren sect, the view of history is full of the excitement of anticipation such as one customarily finds only in the Christian eschatology.[49]

Whatever the cultural predisposition of the Japanese theologians may be, it is undeniable that in every area of their theological discipline today history is being given a position of priority. One of the most illuminating instances of the place of history is to be found in a recent work by Junichi Asano on *The Theology of the Prophets*.[50] As he observes in his introduction, books on the theology of the Old Testament in the past have usually been outlined around theological topics, such as "God," "man," and "salvation." "This," says Asano, "is not in keeping with the formation of the Old Testament, and it is a nonhistorical way of dealing with the problems." Therefore, adopting history as the key category of the Old Testament faith, he addresses himself to such historical topics as "word," "time," "covenant," "election," and "eschatology."

History, according to Asano's interpretation, is the interaction of God's word, which is his personal will, with time. This relation is represented by the covenant, which is the most characteristic aspect of the Old Testament religion and the dominant point of view from which every event is to be interpreted.[51] The sophistication of this view is evident when it is made clear that to call the Old Testament a history does not mean that it is " a mere descriptive record of events. There must be something to integrate and give meaning to events. In this sense, the word creates history." [52] Thus the historical importance of the Old Testament is not in the positive accuracy of its record of events, but in its interpretation. An event is a component of history only when it is attached to some meaning. It is the leading idea of the Old Testament that the mission of Israel was to commend Yahweh as the transcendent, personal will acting behind every vicissitude of history.[53]

Another theologian from whose work some interesting historiographical suggestions are emerging is Tetsutarō Ariga, Hatano's successor at Kyoto University. One of his suggestions is directed against Barth's effort to reduce historical theology to the lowly status of auxiliary to dogmatic theology. Ariga makes a case for the difference between Japan and Europe regarding the significance of historical studies. Europe is just emerging from an era in which historicism forced dogmatic interests into the shade. In Japan, however, historical disciplines are still in a very immature stage of development. Therefore, " the firm establishing of historical theology is necessary for the wholesome progress of theology in Japan." [54]

Another of Ariga's suggestions, which is as yet undeveloped by him, is directed against a tendency in contemporary theology to correlate Biblical categories with ontological categories. Instances of this tendency usually appeal to the words of Yahweh, " I am who I am." God, by that description, is " I am " or " He who is " or " Being itself." Ariga simply reminds the theologian that ontology cannot be the implication of that verse. The Hebrew word *hāyā* communicates the sense of action rather than of being, of history rather than of ontology. A theology that took the active categories of the Biblical faith seriously would not be known as ontology but as *hāyā*tology.[55]

I attempted to show in Chapter II that a mature Biblical concept of history first entered the systematic theology of Japan in Kumano's early work called *Eschatology and Philosophy of History* (1933). There the question is raised as to what it means to say that the foundation of faith is historical. It is not enough to answer that it simply means the faith is real, for there is a form of reality that is not necessarily historical. There is the kind of reality that says two plus two is four. But that is not history. There is also the kind of reality that occurs when a mother fights a wild beast to save the life of her son. That is reality in the category of history.

Now, history occurs when a special event in the past is not buried but influences the present. History has the character of the past but is at the same time present. It is not a mere impression of the past that remains in the present. That would reduce the event to something subjective (*shukanteki*) in the sense of sheer subjectivism. Modern theology fell into this kind of subjectivism when it tried to rediscover the historical Jesus. Nor does the fact that the past is present mean that the past is the cause of the present. Where the present is visible as the causal result of the past we have nature, not history.[56]

As Seiichi Hatano pointed out some time ago[57] it was the merit of the Hebrews to have discovered history. The Hebrew world view was essentially based on vitalistic, volitional terms, where the personal existence of God acts according to his own free will. Hatano, however, has not been so ready to set Hebrew motifs over against Greek motifs as contemporary apologists for Biblical categories tend to do. Plato's theory of " the idea " had value as a contribution to the meaning of history, he claims. It is only that Plato himself did not discover this value. Where the content of the world is regarded in some sense as a repetition of a fundamentally unchanging reality, such as " the idea " in Plato, there is the possibility of understanding the meaning of history. Although that possibility was already present in Plato, he left it undeveloped. For Hatano, therefore, it is " a curious historical fact " that the Greeks possessed a principle for interpreting the meaning of history but did not put it into practice, whereas the Hebrews understood the meaning of history but lacked an adequate concept by which to express it clearly. " The Greek and Hebrew views ought to have supplemented each other." [58]

One of the most exciting illustrations of the coincidence of Greek and Hebrew categories in contemporary Japanese thought is to be found in a work by the late Kiyoshi Miki, a philosopher and free-lance author. His work, *Philosophy of History*, preceded Kumano's *Eschatology and Philosophy of History* by two years. Miki was not a theologian. In fact, he was a professed Buddhist. He once said he hoped to die in the Shinran faith, although it is believed he was more interested in Christianity than in Buddhism. It is an irony of history that he died in prison at the age of forty-seven, long after the Japanese were defeated in the last war. He had been a political prisoner of the Imperial Government for sheltering a key Communist Party member in his home, but was not released when the war ended. In one phase of his philosophical development he had been friendly to Marxism. His philosophical works always bordered upon profoundly Christian themes, however. The irony of his death is that had he lived, he might have become a major influence in interpreting democracy to the new Japan.

His first work was a thesis on Pascal. His most famous work is on *The Logic of the Imagination.* No work in Japanese that has come to my attention seems to contribute so much to the clarification of a central theological concern, however, as Miki's book on *Philosophy of History*. It is not, as the title seems to suggest, an interpretation of the chronological sweep of history but an analysis of the category "history," or what it means to use the word "history." Miki reflects an understanding of the importance to philosophy of the shift away from the classical substance and objectivist categories in the direction of the category of history and subjectivity (*shutai-sei*). He made it clearer than I believe it has yet been made in the West that subjectivity need not infer subjectivism (*shukan-sei*). In subjectivity the cleavage between subject and object is overcome in a third reality known as "meaningful activity," or "actual history." The Japanese, as I have repeatedly shown in this volume, reserve the word *shutai-sei* for this kind of subjectivity.[59] "When we understand that distinction the subjective fact itself (*shutai*) is the real object." [60]

Miki also refused to regard history as a phenomenon on one plane only. When a person limits history to one plane he flirts with immanentalism, continuity thinking, and progress views. These possibilities had to be eliminated by Miki in favor of a dialectical pattern where history is under the necessity of constantly overcoming its own emptiness. Marxism helped him grasp this understanding, but his Marxism was set within the thinking developed in hermeneutical philosophy from Schleiermacher to Dilthey.[61] The doubleness that Miki found in history was not dualistically conceived but dialectically conceived. That is, he considered these elements in history as "dimensions," dialectically related, hence not mutually exclusive.[62]

Miki, a non-Christian, believed that Christianity was the first movement to introduce history in its present sense. History had not even existed hitherto in Greece.[63] However, he did not allow Christians to make this claim a source of pride. He made it clear that Greece lacked a historical consciousness only in the sense in which the modern *bourgeoisie* lacks it, whereas the proletariat today *has* the historical sense.[64]

Less than four years after Heidegger developed the point in his *Sein und Zeit*, Miki organized his own view of history around the conviction that history is a reality oriented primarily toward the future.[65] This future is not simply a possibility of the present for which the present waits. It is a future that is bearing in upon the present to convert the mood of expectation into an act of decisiveness.[66]

Let me attempt to state Miki's very abstract and complicated morphology of history in quite simple terms. Four factors are involved in the notion of history: being, logos, the sources, and actuality. *Being* is history as the event. *Logos* is history as the description of the event. *The sources* are the historical documents that exist between being and logos. *Actuality* is history as presentness and wholeness that gives us not simply our description but our *understanding* of history. Because the sources constitute no real problem in the definition of history, they fall out of the discussion early. The problem that remains is the dialectical correlation of the other three dimensions of history – being, logos, and actuality.

Being is history as it has been made and as it presses upon us from the past with the force of causal inevitability. Man is a slave to history as being. The being of history is history in its systematically objective sense. Logos, on the other hand, is history as description. It is prior to history as being, to the extent that the very being of history already involves some description. But history as being is prior to descriptive history in respect of its occurrence. The being and the logos of history stand to each other as object and subject, respectively. Being is therefore the proper object of ontology and logos of anthropology.

History as actuality, however, is prior to being as its very ground. As such, it overcomes the dialectical relation between object and subject, or being and logos. History as actuality provides the understanding of being in terms of the consciousness of being, not merely in terms of the objective description of being.[67] Here history is being made. Here history, far from being man's overlord, is his creature. Causation, which is the necessary and sufficient explanation of history as being, is not the sufficient explanation of history as actuality. Where the time of being flows from past to future, causally, the time of actuality flows from future to past, teleologically. Therefore history as being exists in the mode of tradition that is handed down from the past, while history as actuality exists in the mode of repetition, drawing the past toward itself in the present.[68] History in its fullest sense begins here, for only in actuality is the question of meaning addressed. History in this sense is an attribute of the relation of the parts to the whole. In being, which is dominated by relations of necessity and genetic causation, where universality is defined in terms of law, there is no such accent upon meaning. In actuality, universality is defined not in terms of law but in terms of wholeness, where meaning is enjoyed.[69] The meaningful history called actuality supplies the ground of history as being.

The usefulness of these distinctions to theology has already been anticipated, especially in the discussions of Kumano and Hatano. The Christian faith deals with a reality that is primarily historical, namely, Jesus of Nazareth as the one in whom God is showing mercy to sinners and calling the world to obedience. Most theologians today agree upon that. How to express that truth theologically without reference to an adequate historiography is more and more the problem of contemporary theology. Access to the knowledge of the Christ-event is in " the sources," that is, in the Sacred Scriptures, which conserve the apostolic testimony to the event, and in the history of the interpretation of those Scriptures. The event has a " being " of its own, the sheer happenedness of the Christ-event, which presses against the continuum of world events from its position in the past. The event also has a logos of its own, which is the apostolic description of the event. Left with only these three dimensions of history, historiography would become a method of negotiating between documentary research, ontology, and anthropology. The negotiations would collapse, however, without the fourth dimension, which is the " actuality " of history. " Actuality " is the meaning of the event for us in the present, which comes to us not as out of the past (although it is there as " being ") but out of the future, providing us a hermeneutically rather than a causally supportive base for our ongoing life. The dimension of historical reality in which the Christian *lives* is history as " actuality."

Conclusion. By its acts of interpretation, the theological mind of Japan has bridged the gap between Jerusalem, Rome, Wittenberg, and Geneva on the one side, and Tokyo on the other. That is an enormous chronological distance, but it shrinks to nothing in the face of such responsible Christian understanding. Time is easier to collapse than space, however. There is a unilateral character to the interpretation of the past. The historian can grasp the past somehow without the past's consent and make it his own. Overcoming spatial distance, however, such as the distance that exists in the present between the traditional churches of the West and the younger churches of the East, requires bilateral encounter. The Japanese have served their apprenticeship at learning their lessons from the West. If Christian history as an ecumenical actuality is to persist in the future, the West must take up its side of the theological partnership and converse with the East.

No Oriental, of course, could issue that invitation. The Japanese people are dominated by one fundamental rule of propriety: they must not imply anything good about themselves. They take their rule so seriously that in order to be sure they will keep it they often say bad things about themselves. It is nothing, therefore, to hear a Japanese theologian describe the intellectual achievements of his church as "the poor theological world of Japan." The same man would say of his wife's superb cooking, "I am sorry to have to invite you to eat this miserable meal!" He is not being rude to his wife or even modest on her behalf. He is simply being what he regards as polite to his guest. Western Christendom, however, need no longer be trapped into indifference to Japanese theology by this oddly urbane self-effacement. The facts are now before us. This volume is offered as extended documentation of a single statement recently made to Karl Barth by Hidenobu Kuwada in a moment when his Oriental mask was down. "The Japanese theologians now stand on their own legs." This was not a declaration of theological independence. It was simply as bold and direct a bid as will ever come from the Japanese themselves for actualization of full citizenship in the Christian church.

Notes

Chapter I

1. Takeshi Fujii, *Collected Works* (*Zenshū*), Vol. VII, pp. 507–508.

2. *An Interim Report on Non-Church Christianity in Japan*, reprinted from the Kwansei Gakuin University Annual Studies, 1958, Nishinomiya, p. 10. This strange definition may partially be explained by an observation Uchimura is known to have made in 1909. He noted that over half the two million Christians in New York City at that time did not attend church. He drew this conclusion: "Therefore I knew that the Non-Church movement is not limited to Japan."

3. Quoted from Uchimura by Masao Sekine, *Non-Church Christianity* (*Mukyōkai Kirisutokyō*), Tokyo, third edition, 1955, pp. 23–24.

4. Tadao Yanaibara, "What Is Non-Churchism?" in *Kashin*, Vol. 19, No. 6, June, 1956, p. 7.

5. Quoted by Sekine, *Non-Church Christianity*, pp. 27–28. The memory of Fujii is not as central to the Non-Church movement today as the memory of Uchimura. The probable reason is that he attempted to go beyond Non-Churchism in a movement he called "New Zionism." His reform determined to add to *Mukyōkai* an emphasis on the future life. As he said, "Non-Churchism + belief in the future life = New Zionism." (*Col-*

lected Works, Vol. VI, pp. 606–607, from an article, "New Zionism," published in April, 1929.) Fujii, of course, was only attempting to remain faithful to the implications of Uchimura's hearty endorsement of the Second Advent movement in the days following the First World War. But when Uchimura later called for a return to the cross as the foundation of Christianity, Fujii persisted in making eschatology central.

6. Yoshitaka Kumano, in *The Christian Weekly* (*Kirisutokyō Shimpō*), March, 1959.

7. Sekine, *Non-Church Christianity*, p. 50. The non-Christian philosopher, Tetsuo Watsuji, has made the point in his work on Kierkegaard (Tokyo, 1917; second edition, 1948, cited here, p. 16) that Uchimura is not really a parallel to Kierkegaard. The reason he gives is that Christianity in Japan is not an *established* religion as it was in Kierkegaard's Denmark. "The idea that Christians should be attacked because they are only playing at Christianity has no relevance in Japan, considering the oppression of its heathen culture upon Christianity."

8. Sekine, *ibid.*, p. 57.

9. Kōkichi Kurosaki, *One Body in Christ* (Eternal Life Press, Kobe, Japan, 1954), p. 48.

10. *Ibid.*, p. 8.

11. Sekine, *Non-Church Christianity*, p. 56.

12. *Ibid.*, p. 52.

13. Tadao Yanaibara, "What Is Non-Churchism?" *Kashin*, Vol. 19, No. 7, July, 1956, p. 7.

14. Sekine, *Non-Church Christianity*, p. 11. A lesser-known problem in ecclesiology in Japan is the small and intentionally obscure group on Ikutsuki Island, at the lower end of Kyushu, called "The Hidden Christians." They represent a body of Roman Catholics founded by Francis Xavier, who went into hiding during the early persecution of Christians two hundred and fifty years ago. They have never come out of hiding. The exigencies of their protracted *incognito* have required them to memorize their liturgy and creeds and to transmit them

orally. They disguise their official clergy, calling priests "father" but bishops "grandfather." They retain their Shinto altars, with ancestor worship as a foreground for their Christian relics and devotional objects, which they conceal behind sliding doors. They camouflage their worship so their funerals, for instance, cannot be distinguished from Buddhist funerals. Pictorial representations of Christ resemble a Japanese court prince, and of God, an emperor. Most striking of all, they have a lay ministry and lay bishops, and no acknowledgment of the pope. They do not observe Holy Communion because when they first went underground they were without the services of an ordained priest, hence learned to get along without the mass. Obviously, they are in communion with no other Christian groups. Their saints include the apostles, Francis Xavier, and their own early martyrs. Now here is a neat ecclesiological question: If this group did finally decide it could trust the Government's promise of freedom of worship and it were to come out of hiding, where in Christendom would it go to find acceptance as a Christian body? (William D. Bray, "The Hidden Christians of Ikutsuki Island," in *Fundamental Problems of Communication* [*Senkyō no Konpon Mondai*], special issue of *Shingaku-Kenkyu*, No. 7, 1958, pp. 425–452. The article is printed in English.)

15. *Ibid.*, p. 39.

16. *Ibid.*, pp. 39–42.

17. Yanaibara, "What Is Non-Churchism?" *Kashin*, Vol. 19, No. 6, June, 1956, p. 7.

18. Saburō Takahashi, "Self-examination and the Future Prospects of Non-Churchism" ("Mukyōkaishugi no hansei to Mirai-tenbō"), *Seisenkai*, 1958, pp. 116–117.

19. Sekine, *Non-Churchism and the Bible* (*Mukyōkaishugi to Seisho*), San-itsu shobō, Shizuoka, 1950, p. 49; and *Non-Church Christianity*, pp. 22 and 33.

20. Sekine, *Non-Church Christianity*, p. 45.

21. *Ibid.*, p. 56.

22. Takahashi, "Self-examination and the Future Prospects

of Non-Churchism," pp. 114–115.

23. Fujii, *Collected Works,* Vol. XII, pp. 25–26, originally written in 1930.

24. Uchimura's evangelistic zeal was second, and " his translation of Christianity into a Japanese idiom " was last in a list of eleven items. Incidental to this, another survey is instructive. In 1951, the National Christian Council of Japan polled students, Christian and non-Christian, of thirty-two universities in Tokyo, regarding their attitude toward religion. From the Christian students' response to the question as to which religious author had impressed them most, Uchimura's name led the list. Luther was second; Barth, third.

25. Fujii, *Collected Works,* Vol. VII, pp. 475–476. The entire article covers pp. 470 to 508.

26. *Ibid.*, p. 490.

27. Gorō Maeda, *Introduction to the New Testament* (*Shinyaku Seisho Gaisetsu*), Tokyo, second edition, 1957, p. 17.

28. *Ibid.*, p. 8.

29. *Ibid.*, p. 9.

30. Sekine, *Non-Churchism and the Bible,* p. 32.

31. Fujii, *Collected Works,* Vol. VI, pp. 504–521.

32. As observed by Tsutomu Oshio in *Modern Japan and Christianity* (*Kindai Nippon to Kirisutokyō*), a Symposium, Hisashi Kuyama, editor, Tokyo, 1956, Vol. II, pp. 23–24.

33. Sekine, *Non-Church Christianity*, p. 54.

34. Sekine, *Non-Churchism and the Bible*, pp. 40 ff.

35. Zenda Watanabe, *The Doctrine of the Scriptures* (*Seisho-ron*), Vol. II, *The Theory of the Interpretation of the Scriptures* (*Kaishaku-ron*), Tokyo, 1954, pp. 90–114.

36. *Ibid.*, p. 101.

37. Zenda Watanabe, *Before and After My Conversion* (*Kaishin to Sono Zengo*), Part I, " My Pilgrimage Into Biblical Studies," Tokyo, 1957, p. 123. Uchimura later came to believe firmly in the Second Coming of Christ, as we have seen earlier in the discussion.

38. *Ibid.*, pp. 172–179.

39. Watanabe, *The Doctrine of the Scriptures,* Vol. II, p. 34.

40. *Ibid.*, p. 286.

41. Zenda Watanabe, *The Place That Produces Hypocrites* (*Gizensha o Dasu Tokoro*), Collection of Sermons, Tokyo, 1958, Sermon 4, "Misunderstanding of Christianity," pp. 41 ff.

42. Tamiko Okamura, *The Bible as Canon* (*Seiten to Shite no Seisho*), Tokyo, 1958, p. 20.

43. *Ibid.*, p. 76.

44. Watanabe, *The Doctrine of the Scriptures*, Vol. II, pp. 344–388.

45. Okamura, *Introduction to the Old Testament* (*Kyūyaku saisho Gairon*), Tokyo, 1955, pp. 17–18.

46. Watanabe, *The Place That Produces Hypocrites*, Sermon 10, "My Gospel," pp. 119–120. Masao Sekine is understandably critical of Watanabe's position. He believes Watanabe gets support for the hermeneutics of structure from the Japanese philosopher Nishida and his "logic of *topos* or place." (*Non-Churchism and the Bible*, p. 23.) However this may be, Watanabe does adduce specific support from Martin Heidegger, who has said in *Sein und Zeit*, "Phenomenological interpretation is not a knowledge of the composition of something but a determination of the structure of its being." There is also acknowledgment of indebtedness to Wilbert W. White, founder of The Biblical Seminary in New York City. Miss Okamura is a product of that school. Cf. Charles R. Eberhardt, *The Bible in the Making of Ministers: The Lifework of Wilbert Webster White* (Association Press, 1949).

47. Watanabe, *The Doctrine of the Scriptures*, Vol. II, p. 85. For the insight into the resolution between faith and works, Watanabe acknowledges dependence upon E. F. Scott.

48. Tsutomu Oshio, in *Modern Japan and Christianity*, Vol. II, p. 306.

Chapter II

1. Yoshitaka Kumano, *Eschatology and Philosophy of History* (*Shūmatsuron to Rekishi-Tetsugaku*), first edition, Tokyo, 1933; sixth edition, referred to in this volume, Tokyo, 1949.

2. *Ibid.*, pp. 38–40.

3. Yoshitaka Kumano, *Outline of Christianity* (*Kirisutokyō Gairon*), Tokyo, 1947.

4. *Ibid.*, pp. 5–7. The influence of Seiichi Hatano may be evident here. For Hatano, the study of a religion presupposes a living body of experience.

5. Yoshitaka Kumano, *Dogmatics* (*Kyōgigaku*), Vol. I, Tokyo, 1954, Vol. II, Tokyo, 1959.

6. Kumano, *Outline of Christianity*, p. 212.

7. *Ibid.*, pp. 236–237.

8. Kumano, *Eschatology*, pp. 37–39.

9. *Ibid.*, pp. 31–34.

10. Kumano, *Dogmatics*, Vol. I, p. 180.

11. *Ibid.*, pp. 235–236.

12. See Kumano, *Eschatology*, pp. 240–241. Kumano instructively calls attention to a shift that occurs in the meaning of history between Martin Heidegger and Friedrich Gogarten. In Heidegger, history means man's being-toward-death. In Gogarten, it means man's being in the presence of an other, an I in the presence of a Thou. In the latter, the significance of one's death is not one's own experience of death but the experience others have who witness that death and stand by that grave. Kumano, following Karl Heim (*Eschatology*, p. 184), does not choose between these views. He combines them. As Heim has said, " The paradoxical delimitation between I and Thou and the limit of death belong together. For the being-to-death is only a particular expression of the way I delimit myself toward the Thou with whom I am related." *Glaube und Denken*, Berlin, 1931, pp. 272–273.

13. Kumano, *Eschatology*, p. 21. Kumano's vigilance about the place of anthropology in theology has increased steadily in his theological development. The second volume of his *Dogmatics* shows a greater caution than his early *Eschatology*. As he comments, in the West anthropology has always been the other side of theology. In the East, however, the distinction between anthropology and theology is rarely made, for the human being is thought to be like " a bubble in the great

ocean" of divinity. (*Dogmatics*, Vol. II, p. 203.) Therefore, it is more than an imitative spirit that directs Kumano to stand with Karl Barth in criticizing anthropological tendencies in theology. In the Orient, with its pantheistic culture, the Barthian warning has a relevance that it does not enjoy even in the West.

14. Kumano, *Eschatology*, p. 168.
15. *Ibid.*, p. 191.
16. *Ibid.*, pp. 192–193.
17. *Ibid.*, p. 194. Cf. *Dogmatics*, Vol. II, pp. 279–281, where Kumano observes that death implies more than a cessation of natural time. As the Bible knows, death is related to sin. The curse of time is not in the finitude alone. Cf. also *Dogmatics*, Vol. I, p. 179: "Man's time is in God's hands. To evade that realization means self-destruction."
18. Kumano, *Eschatology*, p. 201.
19. *Ibid.*, p. 203.
20. Kumano, *Dogmatics*, Vol. II, p. 240.
21. Kumano, *Eschatology*, pp. 48, 51, 264.
22. *Ibid.*, p. 266.
23. *Ibid.*, p. 42.
24. Kumano, *Dogmatics*, Vol. I, p. 179; Vol. II, p. 72.
25. Kumano, *Gospel and World* (*Fukuin to Sekai*), Aug., 1958, "Hope of the End," p. 11.
26. Kumano, *Eschatology*, p. 246.
27. Kumano, *Outline of Christianity*, p. 208.
28. Kumano, *Dogmatics*, Vol. I, p. 31.
29. Kumano, *Outline of Christianity*, pp. 198–211.
30. Kumano, *Dogmatics*, Vol. I, p. 37; cf. also *Outline of Christianity*, pp. 162–167. There is a similar emphasis in the thought of Hatano upon the importance of a synthesis between the life and the learning of a religion.
31. Kumano, *Dogmatics*, Vol. I, pp. 11–12.
32. Kumano, *Outline of Christianity*, p. 118.
33. Kumano, *Dogmatics*, Vol. I, p. 44.
34. Kumano, *Eschatology*, p. 391.

35. Kumano, *Outline of Christianity*, p. 226. "The Non-Church people have stumbled over minor things. Since the church exists within history and society, it cannot avoid being influenced by the taint of secular things. The Non-Church people, however, want their subjective purity, despising the impure elements of church existence. While we can be sympathetic toward them in this, we must transcend them." (*Ibid.*, p. 113.) Tokutarō Takakura, one of Kumano's teachers, had also taken a strong stand against the Non-Church direction. "The essence of the church," he said, "is not system or organization or the people tied to it. The essence of the church is the gospel and faith." (*Evangelical Christianity* [*Fukuinteki Kirisutokyō*], Tokyo, 1927; 1952 edition cited here, p. 143.) If Takakura had not died at the age of forty-nine (in 1934), he would clearly have commanded more attention than can be given him in this volume on theology *today*. The only extended treatment of his theology in English of which I am aware can be found in Charles H. Germany, *Dominant Theological Currents in Japanese Protestant Christianity*, 1920–1958, unpublished doctoral dissertation, Columbia University, 1959, Chapter IV.

36. Kumano, *Dogmatics*, Vol. I, p. 43.

37. Kumano, *Outline of Christianity*, p. 281.

38. *Ibid.*, pp. 282–289. An excellent illustration of Kumano's attitude toward creeds appears in *Dogmatics*, Vol. II, p. 255. He warns against the precipitous tendency in the church today to get rid of the "two natures in one person" formula of the Council of Chalcedon. What is his alternative? The church must understand "the intention" of the formula.

39. Kumano, *Dogmatics*, Vol. I, pp. 45–48.

40. *Ibid.*, p. 97.

41. *Ibid.*, p. 95.

42. *Ibid.*, pp. 103–104.

43. Kumano occasionally misinterprets Bultmann. Kumano is wrong, for instance, to claim that Bultmann knows that the event of revelation cannot express itself except by mythical

symbols. According to Bultmann there *is* a form of expression of the revelation that escapes mythological symbolization. It is called *kērygma.* The critical task of the Biblical exegete is to give priority in exegesis to the *kērygma* and, while not stripping away the myth, at least get to the kerygmatic intention of the myth. Kumano has much company among Western theologians in this misinterpretation.

44. *Ibid.*, p. 71.

45. *The Christian Weekly* (*Kirisutokyō Shimpō*), March, 1959.

46. Cf. Hidenobu Kuwada's *Understanding Theology* (*Shingaku no Rikai*), p. 198, where this was said of Kumano's *Eschatology and Philosophy of History*, and his review of *Dogmatics*, Vol. II, referred to above, where he says the same thing regarding Kumano's dependence upon, yet freedom from Barth.

47. See Chapter III.

48. Kumano, *Dogmatics*, Vol. I, pp. 274–279.

49. *Ibid.*, p. 289.

50. *Ibid.*, pp. 291, 294, and 296–297.

51. *Ibid.*, Vol. II, pp. 17, 36, 52, and 60.

52. *Ibid.*, p. 15.

53. *Ibid.*, p. 52.

54. *Ibid.*, p. 132. Takenosuke Miyamoto has the same insight into the historical meaning of the doctrine of Creation when he points out that natural theology is not to be inferred from a doctrine of Creation. See his *Image of Man in Present-Day Christianity* (*Gendai Kirisutokyō Ningenzō*), Tokyo, 1958, pp. 14 and 94.

55. Kumano, *Dogmatics*, Vol. II, p. 186.

56. *Ibid.*, p. 201.

57. *Ibid.*, pp. 237–238.

58. *Ibid.*, p. 12. In Kumano's *Eschatology*, which was somewhat deliberately directed against the Non-Church movement (see p. 390), Kumano held that the church is not immanent in culture. Rather, it is founded by Jesus Christ, who is an

eschatological event. Therefore, not simply the church itself but even the symbols and sacraments should be regarded as eschatological. (Pp. 355–364.)

59. Kumano, *Dogmatics,* Vol. II, pp. 80–81.

60. *Ibid.,* p. 46.

61. *Ibid.,* I, 308.

62. *Ibid.,* II, p. 109. Cf. also p. 121: "The purpose of God's governance of the world is to set up the conditions for church formation."

63. *Ibid.,* I, pp. 313–321.

64. *Outline of Dialectical Theology* (*Benshōhōteki Shingaku Gairon*), Tokyo, 1932, Chapter IV, "Faith and Ethics."

65. Kumano, *Dogmatics,* Vol. I, pp. 313–314; II, pp. 312, 328–330.

66. Kumano, *Dogmatics,* Vol. I, p. 58.

67. *Ibid.,* p. 260.

Chapter III

1. Kazoh Kitamori, *The Character of the Gospel* (*Fukuin no Seikaku*), Kyoto, 1948, p. 19.

2. "The Pain of God and *Heilsgeschichte*" in *The Theology of the Pain of God* (*Kami no Itami no Shingaku*), Tokyo, fourth edition, the edition herein referred to unless otherwise specified, 1946, Chapter II.

3. Kazoh Kitamori, *Theology Today* (*Konnichi no Shingaku*), Tokyo, 1950.

4. Kitamori, *The Character of the Gospel,* p. 102.

5. Kitamori, *The Theology of the Pain of God,* p. 44.

6. Among those in Japan who state the case for the traditional view of God's impassibility most persuasively is Yoshio Noro. "If God suffers for our salvation," he comments, "why should we not give up our salvation? The suffering God will completely deprive us of the blessed happiness in our fellowship with him." (*The Theology of Friedrich von Hügel,* privately published paper, p. 41. The original Japanese version of this paper appears in *Journal of Christian Studies* [*Kirisu-*

tokyō Ronshū], No. 6, Feb., 1958. Cf. also Noro's unpublished doctoral dissertation, *Impassibilitas Dei*, Part I, pp. 29–102, on Kitamori's view. Union Theological Seminary, New York, 1955.)

7. Kitamori, *The Theology of the Pain of God*, p. 69.

8. Kitamori, *Theology Today*, p. 4.

9. *Ibid.*, p. 145.

10. Kitamori, *The Theology of the Pain of God*, p. 41.

11. Kitamori, *The Character of the Gospel*, p. 43; *The Justification of God*, Peter T. Forsyth; cf. p. 151: "Sin is the death of God. Die sin must or God." The influence of Forsyth seems to have entered Japanese theology through the teaching of Tokutarō Takakura, one-time president of a Presbyterian theological seminary in Tokyo, who studied in Great Britain from 1921 to 1924. Takakura was a watershed in Japanese theology between the wars, mediating between the missionary-inspired extremes of liberalism and fundamentalism.

12. Kitamori, *The Theology of the Pain of God*, p. 149; *The Character of the Gospel*, p. 56; *Theology Today*, pp. 92–93.

13. Kazoh Kitamori, *The Logic of Salvation* (*Kyūsai no Ronri*), Tokyo, 1953, p. 32.

14. Kitamori, *The Character of the Gospel*, pp. 38–39.

15. Kitamori, *The Theology of the Pain of God*, p. 189.

16. *Ibid.*, pp. 32 ff., 51 f., 58 ff., and 70.

17. *Ibid.*, p. 129.

18. Kitamori, *The Logic of Salvation*, pp. 136–138. The main thing about this story is the offering of pain, just as the main thing about the story of the three Wise Men is the offering of gold, frankincense, and myrrh (p. 139).

19. Kitamori, *The Theology of the Pain of God*, pp. 124–129; *The Logic of Salvation*, where the Christian attitude toward social need is held to be profounder than the Marxist attitude on the basis of this exegesis of the Matt., ch. 26, incident. "Jesus commanded the people to put attention to him above their concern for the oppressed people of society." This

surprising fact, says Kitamori, requires a new look at the significance of the gospel. (Cf. pp. 99–100.)

20. Kitamori, *The Theology of the Pain of God*, pp. 52–57.
21. Kitamori, *The Character of the Gospel*, p. 41.
22. Kitamori, *The Theology of the Pain of God*, p. 180.
23. Kitamori, *The Character of the Gospel*, p. 74.
24. *Ibid.*, pp. 74–76.
25. *Ibid.*, p. 84.
26. See his book *Is Christ God?* (*Kirisuto wa Kami Ka*), Tokyo, 1955. The discussion between Odagiri and Kitamori appeared in 1956 in the Y.M.C.A. magazine, *The Pioneer* (*Kaitakusha*). One might make the case that theological seriousness in Japanese Christendom had its birth in a similar Christological debate between two popular and learned pastors in Tokyo in 1901. The Presbyterian Masahisa Uemura, of the Ichibancho Church, defended a traditional view of the deity of Christ against Danjō Ebina, Congregational pastor of the Hongō Church. Ebina emphasized the humanity of Christ as the sign through which we know God. Uemura affirmed that Christ is God, hence a legitimate object of man's worship. Ebina preached Christ as a model or example; Uemura preached Christ as God's atonement for man's sin. There is something symbolic in the fact that Ebina carried on his argument through his journal, *Shinjin*, meaning "New Man," Uemura through his own journal, *Fukuin Shimpō*, meaning "Evangelist." Uemura was a poor orator and writer compared to Ebina, yet over a period of time Uemura is said to have attracted the larger congregations. (Hidenobu Kuwada, *Understanding Theology* [*Singaku no Rikai*], p. 407.)
27. Kitamori, *The Logic of Salvation*, p. 69. Yoshitaka Kumano has criticized the Western theologian, Oscar Cullmann, in a similar vein, for failing to enter into "the theological depth" of Scripture. (*Dogmatics*, Vol. II, p. 75.)
28. Kitamori, *The Theology of the Pain of God*, fifth edition, Tokyo, 1958, p. 9. Kitamori indicates in this same place, however, that the Colloquial Bible itself recognizes that *hāmāh*

can be translated as "pain," for it does so in at least two other places, Jer. 48:36 and Ps. 55:17. Dr. Eugene A. Nida, Secretary of the translations department of the American Bible Society, has pointed out that there is a word for "love" in the language of the Miskito Indians of Nicaragua that literally means "pain in the heart."

29. Kitamori, *The Theology of the Pain of God*, fourth edition, p. 214.

30. *Ibid.*, pp. 174 ff.

31. William Adams Brown, *Christian Theology in Outline*, p. 111, quoted on p. 88 of *Theology Today*, Kitamori.

32. Hastings Rashdall, *The Idea of Atonement in Christian Theology*, p. 430, quoted on p. 88 of *Theology Today*, Kitamori.

33. Kitamori, *The Character of the Gospel*, pp. 126–129; *The Theology of the Pain of God*, pp. 14 ff.

34. Kitamori, *The Character of the Gospel*, p. 43.

35. Kitamori, *The Theology of the Pain of God*, pp. 20–21.

36. Kitamori, *The Logic of Salvation*, p. 20.

37. Kitamori, *The Theology of the Pain of God*, pp. 197–199. In the preface to the latest edition of this work, the fifth edition of 1958, Kitamori compares his strategy with the theological work of Athanasius and Luther. Both formed their theologies outside the universal church, yet eventually achieved recognition by the church. This movement from the outside to the inside is the sign of a doctrinal innovator. (P. 8.)

38. Kitamori, *The Theology of the Pain of God*, p. 60.

39. Kitamori, *The Character of the Gospel*, p. 80; *The Theology of the Pain of God*, pp. 45 ff. Kumano sides with Barth against Kitamori, therefore, when he claims that "there is no contradiction in the Trinity. There is only eternal, peaceful fellowship between the three Persons." *Dogmatics*, Vol. I, p. 169.

40. Kitamori, *The Character of the Gospel*, p. 50.

41. *Ibid.*

42. Kitamori, *Theology Today*, p. 20.

43. *Ibid.*

44. As illustrated in modern theology in the case of Ritschl, for instance. *Ibid.*, p. 64.

45. Kitamori, *The Theology of the Pain of God*, p. 27.

46. *Ibid.*, p. 147. As Kitamori says in the fifth edition, p. 9, the critics of his position can find nowhere in his book a reference to the suffering of the Father.

47. Kitamori, *Theology Today*, p. 22.

48. In Kitamori's first book, *Lord of the Cross*, p. 24, quoted on p. 44 of *The Character of the Gospel.*

49. Kitamori, *The Character of the Gospel*, pp. 27–28. Cf. Hajime Tanabe on the logic of neither/nor in *Philosophy as Repentance* (*Zange-dō to shite no Tetsugaku*), Tokyo, 1945, p. 63.

50. Kitamori, *The Character of the Gospel*, p. 35.

51. Kitamori, *The Theology of the Pain of God*, p. 76; cf. also p. 132.

52. Kitamori, *The Character of the Gospel*, pp. 32, 33.

53. Kitamori, *The Logic of Salvation*, p. 109.

54. *The Prophets and Their Times*, J. M. Powis Smith, p. 191, cited in Kitamori, *The Theology of the Pain of God*, p. 81.

55. The materials of this paragraph are drawn from Kitamori's chapter on "The Marburg Colloquy," in *The Character of the Gospel*, pp. 178–191.

56. Kitamori, *The Theology of the Pain of God*, pp. 104, 117, 121 f.

57. *Ibid.*, Preface, p. 3.

CHAPTER IV

1. *Japanese Idealists* (*Nippon no Kannenronsha*), by Shinichi Funayama, Tokyo, 1956, p. 193.

2. *Reason and Revelation* (*Risei to Keiji*), "The Problem of Philosophy of Religion in Theology," by Enkichi Kan, Tokyo, 1953, p. 19.

3. Seiichi Hatano, *Philosophy of Religion* (*Shūkyō Tetsugaku*), *Collected Works* (*Zenshū*), Vol. IV, p. 187.

4. *Ibid.*, p. 27.

5. Shōgo Yamaya, *Modern Japan and Christianity* (*Kindai Nippon to Kirisutokyō*), Tokyo, 1956, p. 297.

6. Seiichi Hatano, *Time and Eternity* (*Toki to Eien*), *Collected Works* (*Zenshū*), Vol. V.

7. Hatano, *Philosophy of Religion*, pp. 182–183.

8. Hatano, *Time and Eternity*, p. 12. In the works of Yoshitaka Kumano, which rely so heavily on eschatological categories, no such consistent distinction is made between *mirai* and *shōrai*. However, to accommodate the eschatological meaning of future, Kumano himself has employed a distinctive use in the word *yukusue*, which is translated " future " but literally means " the ultimate edge of our process." See his *Eschatology* (*Shūmatsuron to Rekishi-Tetsugaku*), sixth edition, Tokyo, 1949, pp. 264–265.

9. Hatano, *Time and Eternity*, p. 15.

10. *Ibid.*, pp. 57 f.

11. *Ibid.*, p. 19.

12. *Ibid.*, see especially pp. 14 and 136; *Philosophy of Religion*, p. 188. Cf. Tetsuo Watsuji, *Climate* (*Fūdo*), Tokyo, first edition, 1935, edition cited here, 1949, p. 232: " Love is not a means to the end of desire, but desire a means to the end of love."

13. Hatano, *Time and Eternity*, p. 139.

14. Hatano, *Philosophy of Religion*, p. 153.

15. *Ibid.*, p. 85.

16. *Ibid.*, p. 47.

17. *Ibid.*, p. 152.

18. Hatano, *Time and Eternity*, pp. 72–73.

19. *Ibid.*, p. 81.

20. *Ibid.*

21. *Ibid.*, p. 84.

22. Hatano, *Philosophy of Religion*, p. 250.

23. Hatano, *Time and Eternity*, pp. 195 ff. Martin Heidegger, who uses the concept of future in much the same way in which Hatano uses *shōrai*, is criticized by Hatano because he

attempts to understand the future of the human being without reference to the real other that Hatano identifies as God. (*Philosophy of Religion*, p. 204.) Takenosuke Miyamoto makes a similar point in his recent work, *The Image of Man in Present-Day Christianity* (*Gendai Kirisutokyō Ningenzō*), Tokyo, 1958, p. 72: "Existentialism will never arrive at true selfhood by way of atheism."

24. Hatano, *Time and Eternity*, pp. 150 ff.

25. Hatano's criticism of Nygren himself is that his elaboration of *agapē* is simply a restatement of a truth uncovered by Karl Holl, the German historian, ten years earlier. (Hatano, *Philosophy of Religion*, p. 198.)

26. *Ibid.*, p. 47.

27. *Ibid.*, p. 223.

28. *Ibid.*, pp. 68 ff.

29. Hatano, *Time and Eternity*, p. 155. Kumano seems to have incorporated this understanding of Hatano into his own position. As he says, "By holy separation God wants a new kind of communion with man. Holiness is the way the Holy Spirit expresses God's transcendence." (*Dogmatics* [*Kyōgigaku*], Vol. I, Tokyo, 1954, p. 254.)

30. Hatano, *Time and Eternity*, p. 155.

31. *Ibid.*, p. 159.

32. Hatano, *Philosophy of Religion*, p. 60.

33. *Ibid.*, pp. 197–198.

34. Friedrich Gogarten, *Ich glaube an den dreieinigen Gott*, Jena, 1926. Kitarō Nishida, the first Japanese philosopher to do philosophy in the Western style and yet to retain the Oriental, Buddhistic point of view, was Hatano's senior colleague at Kyoto University. In his most outstanding work, *The Self-conscious Limitation of Nothingness* (*Mu no Jikakuteki Gentei*), he has a moving section entitled "I and Thou" that is explicit in its dependence upon Gogarten. The volume was first published in 1932. It can be found in his *Collected Works* (*Zenshū*), Vol. VI, Tokyo, 1948. Where Hatano and Gogarten relate man's historical reality to his encounter with the

positive reality of God, Nishida attempts to achieve the same by the encounter with " the absolute other seen at the depth of our self." Where the God of Gogarten and Hatano is met as out of the future, the God of Nishida is the " past Thou." " All that is real is grounded in this I-Thou relationship " where " the present I encounters the past Thou. Herein lies the reality of history as the self-conscious limitation of nothingness."

35. Hatano, *Time and Eternity*, p. 174.

36. Hatano, *Philosophy of Religion*, p. 274.

37. *Ibid.*, pp. 253 f.

38. *Ibid.*, p. 121. Cf. Kumano, *Eschatology*, pp. 350–351, where he takes the position that if Christian love is *agapē*, then two things follow. First, it presupposes an absolute distinction between I and Thou. Love does not establish itself in a pantheistic world view. *Agapē* destroys one's subjective self-sufficiency. It is a sentence of death to our egotism. Second, it also poses a venturesome decision, a venture in God's love for sinners. Venture does not come when we think everything in terms of values. Venture comes when we love the unworthy. Cf. also Kumano, *Dogmatics*, Vol. I, p. 202: " By God's free grace, we the creatures are called ' thou ' out of nothing. That makes us really personal. The fact that man becomes personal, therefore, is an eschatological fact."

39. Hatano, *Time and Eternity*, pp. 150 ff.

40. *Ibid.*, p. 181.

41. *Ibid.*, pp. 183–185.

42. Hatano, *Philosophy of Religion*, p. 204.

43. The religious significance of existential symbolism is effectively interpreted in a volume called *Philosophy as Symbol* (*Shōchō to shite no Tetsugaku*), by Takenosuke Miyamoto, Tokyo, 1948. A great many of Hatano's characteristic theses are also carried out by Miyamoto in his *Image of Man in Present-Day Christianity*. Another Japanese theologian whose work is oriented toward Hatano's position is Katsumi Matsumura of Kwansei Gakuin University. See especially his *Communion with God* and a series of articles in *Shingaku-Kenkyū*

on the theme, "Logic of the Gospel," No. 3, Sept., 1954; No. 4, Nov., 1955; and No. 6, June, 1957.

44. Hatano's distinction between symbol and allegory is suggestive of Kumano's distinction between *denshō* and *dentō* and of Bultmann's distinction between *kērygma* and myth.

45. Hatano, *Time and Eternity*, p. 214.

46. *Ibid.*, pp. 227–228.

CHAPTER V

1. Jisaburō Matsuki, *Man and Christ* (*Ningen to Kirisuto*), Tokyo, 1955, pp. 76–83.

2. Kumano, *Dogmatics* (*Kyōgigaku*), Vol. I, Tokyo, 1954, pp. 117–123.

3. *Ibid.*, Vol. II, Tokyo, 1959, p. 247.

4. *Shōchō to shite no Tetsugaku*, Tokyo, 1948.

5. *Ibid.*, pp. 19 f. and 36.

6. Takenosuke Miyamoto, *The Image of Man in Present-Day Christianity* (*Gendai Kirisutokyō Ningenzō*), Tokyo, 1958, pp. 156–157.

7. *Risei to Keiji*, Tokyo.

8. *Ibid.*, p. 8.

9. *Ibid.*, p. 33.

10. *Ibid.*, p. 127.

11. *Ibid.*, p. 168.

12. *Ibid.*, p. 161.

13. *Ibid.*, pp. 158–187.

14. *Ibid.*, p. 19.

15. Seiichi Hatano, *Collected Works* (*Zenshū*), Vol. III, "Introduction to Religious Philosophy," pp. 142–143.

16. Kazuo Mutō, *Philosophy of Religion* (*Shūkyō Tetsugaku*), Tokyo, 1955, pp. 119–120, 156, 160.

17. *Evangelical Christianity* (*Fukuinteki Kirisutokyō*), Tokyo, first published in 1927, this edition 1952, p. 151.

18. See Ernest Best, *The Influence of Political and Economic Factors Upon the Development of Protestant Christianity in Japanese Society* 1859–1911, unpublished doctoral dissertation, Drew University, 1958.

19. On the basis of this puzzling fact, Prof. Antei Hiyane has issued an urgent call to his fellow Christians to invest more earnestly in efforts to understand the other faiths. " A Strategy for the Christian Ministry in Heathen [*sic*] Japan," *Japan Christian Quarterly*, April, 1958, pp. 140–144.

20. Yasumasa Ōshima, *The Ultimately Limited Situations in the History of the Ethics of Existence* (*Jitsuzon-rinri no Rekishiteki Kyōi*), Tokyo, 1956. Cf. Oshima's own summary of his work in *The Japan Science Review*, Vol. 9, 1958, p. 105: " At last I convince [*sic*] with Kierkegaard, that Jesus Christ is the highest and deepest existence in European spiritual history. . . . To follow him will be the very way to subdue our modern nihilism."

21. See Kazuo Mutō, " Present-Day Task of Religious Existence," in *Kierkegaard Studies* (*Kierkegaard Kenkyū*), edited by Takahiko Sasaki, Tokyo, 1950, pp. 31–35. Cf. also his *Philosophy of Religion*, pp. 70–116; Kumano, *Dogmatics*, Vol. II, Tokyo, 1959, p. 175; Ha Tai Kim, " Nishida and Royce," *Philosophy East and West*, January, 1952, pp. 18 ff.

22. *Christianity in Asia* (*Ajiya ni okeru Kirisutokyō*), edited by H. R. Fox and Kanō Yamamoto, Tokyo, 1955, pp. 117 ff.

23. Kitamori, *The Logic of Salvation* (*Kyūsai no Ronri*), Tokyo, 1953, pp. 8–9.

24. Kan, *Reason and Revelation*, p. 169.

25. Kano Yamamoto, *Eschatology* (*Shūmatsu no Shisō*), Tokyo, 1948, p. 252.

26. Kitamori, *The Logic of Salvation*, pp. 8–10.

27. *Ibid.*, p. 76.

28. Kitamori, *The Character of the Gospel*, (*Fukuin no Seikaku*), Kyoto, 1948, p. 131.

29. Kitamori, *The Logic of Salvation*, pp. 105–106.

30. Hidenobu Kuwada, " Problem of Proclamation in Japan " (" Nippon ni Okeru Senkyō "), *Journal of Theology* (*Shingaku*), Oct., 1950, p. 17.

31. Watanabe, *The Place That Produces Hypocrites* (*Gizensha o Dasu Tokoro*), Collection of Sermons. Tokyo, 1958, Sermon I, by the same title.

32. Drawn from Kumano's *Outline of Dialectical Theology* (*Benshōhōteki Shingaku Gairon*), Tokyo, 1932, Ch. IV.

33. Tetsuo Watsuji, *Ethics as the Study of Man* (*Ningen no gaku toshiteno Rinri-gaku*), Tokyo, first edition 1934; second edition in 1946. Second edition cited here.

34. In the written character for "man," 人間, pronounced *ningen*, it is believed by some that the concept of man as "between man and man" is pictographically suggested.

35. Tetsuo Watsuji, *Søren Kierkegaard*, Tokyo, first edition 1917; revised edition, cited here, 1948, p. 17. The preface was written in 1948.

36. Fox and Yamamoto, eds., *Christianity in Asia*, p. 39.

37. Yamamoto, *Eschatology*, p. 259.

38. As Katsumi Matsumura has acknowledged in "Logic of the Gospel," *Shingaku-Kenkyū*, No. 4, Nov., 1955, p. 14. Cf. also Kazuo Mutō, "Present-Day Task of Religious Existence," p. 28; cf. also Kitamori on Tanabe's social philosophy in *The Character of the Gospel.*

39. Cf. Masao Takenaka, *Relation of Protestantism to Social Problems in Japan*, 1900–1941, unpublished doctoral dissertation, Yale University, 1954, p. 89.

40. Fujii, *Collected Works*, (*Zenshū*), Vol. IV, p. 301.

41. Tadao Yanaibara, *Convictions and Thoughts* (*Shuchō to Zuisō*), Tokyo, 1957, p. 141.

42. *Ibid.*, p. 161.

43. Kanzō Uchimura, *Collected Works* (*Zenshū*), Vol. V, p. 276, 1903, and Vol. XIV, p. 151, 1900, respectively.

44. Kanzō Uchimura, *Zenshin*, Vol. XII, p. 429, an article on "The Basic Problem of Nations," in 1908. I am indebted to the thesis by Masao Takenaka for these citations from Uchimura. *Op. cit.*, pp. 118–119, 124.

45. Enkichi Kan, "The Direction of Social Christianity and Its Theology," *The Pioneer* (*Kaitakusha*), April, 1931, p. 30. Cited, with some changes in wording, from Takenaka, *op. cit.*, p. 243.

46. Matsuki, *Man and Christ*, p. 240.

47. Mutō, *Philosophy of Religion*, pp. 162–163.

48. Cf. Langdon Warner, *The Enduring Art of Japan*, Evergreen, 1952: "The Japanese emphasized man and what happened in the material world at a particular time."

49. See "Buddhist and Taoist Interpretations of History," in *Studies in the Christian Religion* (*Kirisutokyō Kenkyū*), Kyoto, Vol. XXX, No. 4, Oct., 1957, pp. 25–32.

50. *Israel Yogensha no Shingaku*, Tokyo, 1955.

51. *Ibid.*, p. 146.

52. *Ibid.*, p. 142.

53. Cf. also Masao Sekine's work, *The Uniqueness of God in the Old Testament* (*Kyūyaku ni okeru Kami no Dokuitsusei*), especially the appendix on "The Problem of History in Old Testament Theology," 1947. This work was the first to introduce Rudolf Bultmann's demythologizing project into Japanese theology.

54. Tetsutarō Ariga, "What Makes Historical Theology a Theology?" *Studies in the Christian Religion*, Vol. XXVIII, Nos. 3, 4, Oct., 1955, p. 18. Ken Ishihara, church historian, attributes the beginning of theological self-consciousness in Japan to the appearance forty years ago of the first complete *History of Christianity* (*Kirisutokyō Shi*) by En Kashiwai. See Ishihara's article in *Gospel and World* (*Fukuin to Sekai*), Sept., 1959.

55. Tetsutarō Ariga, "Being and Hāyā" ("Yū to Hāyā"), *ibid.*, Vol. XXX, Nos. 1, 2.

56. *Ibid.*, pp. 36, 37.

57. Seiichi Hatano, "Greek and Hebrew Thinking Concerning the Meaning of History," *Collected Works* (*Zenshū*), Vol. III, from a lecture delivered at Kyoto University in 1922.

58. *Ibid.*, p. 278.

59. Kiyoshi Miki, *Philosophy of History* (*Rekishi-Tetsugaku*), Tokyo, 1947, p. 89.

60. *Ibid.*, p. 69.

61. *Ibid.*, pp. 130 and 215 ff.

62. *Ibid.*, pp. 100–138; cf. my *The Hinge of History* (Charles

Scribner's Sons, 1959), Ch. I, "Dimensions of History."

63. Miki, *Philosophy of History*, p. 46.

64. *Ibid.*, p. 47.

65. *Ibid.*, p. 164.

66. *Ibid.*, p. 32. One might have concluded that Miki learned this attitude toward "future" from Hatano, who was his teacher. One possible sign that he did not is that he fails to make the distinction between *mirai* and *shōrai* that Hatano insisted upon.

67. *Ibid.*, p. 213.

68. *Ibid.*, pp. 164 ff.

69. *Ibid.*, pp. 86–87.

INDEX I

Names and Subjects

NAMES

Anselm, 94
Ariga, Tetsutarō, 155 f., 183
Aristotle, 103
Arius, 91
Asano, Junichi, 154
Athanasius, 92, 175
Augustine, 31, 41, 107, 115
Aulén, Gustav, 94

Barth, Karl, 39, 48, 50, 63 f., 66 ff., 75, 77, 90, 104, 127 ff., 131 ff., 143, 148, 155, 162, 169, 171
Bashō, 139
Benedict, Ruth, 11
Bergson, Henri, 107
Best, Ernest, 180
Bray, William, 165
Brown, William Adams, 87, 175
Brunner, Emil, 20, 131 ff., 140
Buber, Martin, 41, 118 ff.
Bultmann, Rudolf, 62, 67, 170 f., 180, 183

Camus, Albert, 108
Cullmann, Oscar, 174

Dante, 105, 114
Darwin, Charles, 37
Dengyō, 153 f.
Diem, Hermann, 63
Dilthey, Wilhelm, 39, 158
Diodorus of Tarsus, 37
Doi, Masatoshi, 153 f.
Dostoevsky, Fydor, 104

Eberhardt, Charles, 167
Ebina, Danjō, 174

Feuerbach, Ludwig, 118
Forsyth, Peter T., 78, 173
Fox, H. R., 181 f.
Froude, James Anthony, 139

Fujii, Takeshi, 17, 22, 27 f., 32, 149, 163 f., 166, 182
Funayama, Shinichi, 176

Germany, Charles, 170
Gogarten, Friedrich, 47, 49 f., 54, 118 f., 168, 178 f.
Gunther, John, 11

Hatano, Seiichi, 11 f., 55, 99, 100 ff., 129, 132 ff., 145, 155 ff., 161, 168 f., 176 ff., 183 f.
Hegel, G. W. F., 74, 105, 112
Heidegger, Martin, 34, 39, 74, 103 f., 107, 159, 167 f.
Heim, Karl, 168
Herrmann, Wilhelm, 80, 130
Hiyane, Antei, 181
Holl, Karl, 84, 178
Hugh of St. Victor, 36
Husserl, Edmund, 39

Ishihara, Ken, 183
Ishikawa, 141

Kagawa, Toyohiko, 149
Kan, Enkichi, 130, 133, 150, 181 f.
Kashiwai, En, 183
Kierkegaard, Sören, 19 f., 104 f., 133, 147 f., 164, 181
Kim, Ha Tai, 181
Kitamori, Kazoh, 12, 65, 73 ff., 139 ff., 142 f., 145, 172 ff., 181 f.
Kumano, Yoshitaka, 12, 23, 46 ff., 90, 124 f., 128 f., 145, 156 f., 164, 167 ff., 174, 177, 179 f., 181 f.
Kurosaki, Kōkichi, 23 f., 27, 94 f., 164
Kuwada, Hidenobu, 63, 162, 171, 174, 181
Kuyama, Hisashi, 166

Lewis, Edwin, 12
Luther, Martin, 20, 26, 31, 41, 61, 77, 83, 85 f., 97 f., 175

Maeda, Gorō, 31, 166
Matsuki, Jisaburō, 128, 151, 180, 182
Matsumura, Katsumi, 179, 182
Miki, Kiyoshi, 99, 157, 183 f.
Miyamoto, Takenosuke, 129, 132, 171, 178 ff.
Motoori, Norinaga, 88
Mutō, Kazuo, 133 f., 180 ff.

Nida, Eugene A., 175
Niebuhr, Reinhold, 142, 148
Nishida, Kitarō, 138, 178 f., 181
Norman, W. H. H., 19, 28, 163
Noro, Yoshio, 11, 172 f.
Nygren, Anders, 115, 178

Odagiri, Nobuo, 84, 174
Okamura, Tamiko, 41, 167
Ōshima, Yasumasa, 137 f., 181
Oshio, Tsutomu, 166 f.

Pascal, Blaise, 105, 158
Plato, 103, 114, 157

Rashdall, Hastings, 87, 175
Ritschl, Albrecht, 80
Royce, Josiah, 181

Sartre, Jean-Paul, 108 f.
Sasaki, Takahiko, 181
Schleiermacher, Friedrich, 80, 105, 158
Sekine, Masao, 23, 25, 33, 163 f., 166 f., 183
Shiga, Naoya, 148
Smith, J. M. Powis, 176

Taishi, Shōtoku, 87
Takahashi, Saburō, 27, 165
Takakura, Tokutarō, 134, 170, 173
Takenaka, Masao, 182
Tanabe, Hajime, 75, 148, 182
Theodore of Mopsuestia, 37
Tillich, Paul, 142
Tolstoy, Leo, 151
Torrance, T. F., 63
Troeltsch, Ernst, 47, 49, 130

Uchimura, Kanzō, 18 f., 21 f., 26 ff., 32, 34, 37, 135, 150, 163, 166, 182
Uemura, Masahisa, 50, 78, 101, 174

Warner, Langdon, 183
Watanabe, Zenda, 12, 35 ff., 60 ff., 124, 144, 166 f., 181
Watsuji, Tetsuo, 12, 105, 146 f., 151, 164, 177, 182
Wesley, John, 37, 41
White, Wilbur W., 167
Wobbermin, G., 130

Xavier, Francis, 142, 164 f.

Yamamoto, Kanō, 142, 148, 181 f.
Yamaya, Shōgo, 103 f., 177
Yanaibara, Tadao, 20, 22 f., 27, 150, 163 f., 182

Zwingli, Huldreich, 97

SUBJECTS

Aesthetics, 139 ff.
Agapē, 102, 105, 114 ff., 118, 120 f., 132, 145, 179
Allegory, 36, 45, 123, 180
Analogia doloris, 89 f., 93
Analogia entis, 89 f.
Anthropology, 52, 67 ff., 113, 118, 147, 160 f., 168. *See also* Man
Apologetics, 103, 129 f., 142 f.
Arianism, 92
Art, 14, 153

Atheism, 178
Atonement, 78, 94 ff., 98

Bible, 17 ff., 28 f., 56, 60. *See also* Hermeneutics
as Canon 30, 32 f., 35 ff., 39, 59, 61, 125, 166 ff.
infallibility of, 37
inspiration of, 60
scientific study of, 31, 39 ff., 62
tradition and, 40 f., 58, 60
Buddhism, 74 f., 87 f., 113, 117, 123, 134, 136, 142, 153, 165, 178, 183
Christianity and, 55, 71, 87, 153
Nichiren, 154
Shinran, 142, 157
Zen, 139

Calvinism, 66, 137
Chalcedon, 58, 170
Christology, 56, 59, 65, 68 ff., 91 ff., 170, 174
Church, 9, 23 f., 26, 35, 40, 44, 46 ff., 50, 56 f., 66, 69, 97, 125, 137, 143 f., 171 f., 175. *See also* Non-Church Movement
authority of, 30
continuity of, 58
mediation of, 46 ff., 57
as symbol, 96
Communication 46, 73, 122, 134, 142 f., 165
Community, 112, 119, 138, 145, 147, 149
Cosmology. *See* Creation; Nature
Creation, 29 f., 63, 66 f., 116 f., 122, 171
Creeds, 24, 56, 59
Culture, 100, 105, 110 ff., 118, 129 f., 134, 142 ff., 147, 171
Christianity and, 134 ff.

Death, 49, 51 ff., 55, 112 ff., 123 f., 146, 168 f.
Decision, 54 f., 148, 179
Demythologizing, 62, 170 f., 183
Denominationalism, 32, 60 ff. *See also* Ecumenicity
Dialectic, 75, 95 f., 105, 154, 158
Dialectical theology, 70, 145 ff., 172
Docetism, 92

Ecumenicity, 9 ff., 15, 50, 57, 60, 97, 162, 164
Election, 55, 66, 68, 70
Epithumia, 105, 177
Erōs, 82, 105, 110 ff., 114, 118
Eschatology, 37 f., 47, 50 ff., 54 ff., 70, 79, 156 f., 164, 177, 179
Buddhist, 153
Eternal life, 51, 69. *See also* Immortality

Eternity, 104, 113 ff., 123. *See also* Love: time of
Ethics, 44, 64, 70 ff., 81, 98, 120, 121 ff., 136, 143 ff., 173
Evangelism, 103, 124, 135 ff.
Existentialism, 33 f., 48, 50, 94, 104, 108 f., 137, 142, 148, 178 f., 181
  ecclesiological, 49 ff., 65

Faith, 54, 57, 59, 120 f., 123, 129
Feudalism, 119, 135 f.
Forgiveness, 79, 82, 85, 92
Fundamentalism, 62, 173
Future, 114, 159, 177, 184. *See also* Time
  two words for, 107 f.

God, 29, 52 ff., 63, 66, 114, 155, 178. *See also* Trinity
  eschatology and, 51
  freedom of, 156, 179
  hiddenness of, 86, 123
  in history, 54
  holiness of, 116 ff., 178
  immanence of, 81
  impassibility of, 76, 172 f.
  Kingdom of, 23, 148
  knowledge of, 127 ff., 133, 174
  mercy of, 87, 146, 161
  pain of, 73 ff., 145, 172 ff.
  power of, 117
  righteousness of, 94 ff.
  time and, 101, 154
  transcendence of, 178
  wrath of, 76, 78 ff., 82, 95
Grace, 30, 57, 70, 77, 122
Guilt, 52

Haiku, 73, 139
*Hāyā*tology, 155 f.
Hermeneutics, 36 ff., 39 ff., 42 ff., 61, 74, 84 ff., 158, 161, 167, 174
"Hidden Christians, The," 164 f.
History, 49, 52, 54, 62, 66, 119, 139, 152 ff., 156, 158, 168, 183
  church, 25, 69, 155, 183
  community and, 112, 119
  dimensions of, 158 ff., 183 f.
  eschatology and, 47, 49, 51 ff., 145
  nature and, 66, 152, 156
Holiness group, 21, 37 f.
Holy Spirit, 36 f., 51, 90

Idealists, British, 75
Image of God, 29, 69
Immortality, 51, 53, 55, 69, 123 f.
Incarnation, 30, 51, 55 f., 84, 92
Individuality, 32, 110, 121
Irony, 100, 109, 111, 144, 157

Jesus Christ, 29 f., 33, 49, 55 f., 68 ff., 84, 171
Judaism, 31, 96
Justification, 58

Kairos, 154

Language, 111
- Chinese, 135
- German, 14, 34, 52, 74
- English, 33, 52
- Japanese, 9 ff., 33, 52, 74, 107 ff., 110, 119, 139, 147

Law, 43, 95
Liberalism, 75, 77, 80, 87, 130, 149, 173
Love, 53, 87, 119 f., 129, 146, 175, 177, 179
- of God, 81
- monism of, 77, 79
- of neighbor, 81, 98, 151
- three orders of, 79
- time of, 100 ff., 115. *See also* Eternity

Lutheranism, 77

Man, 69, 106, 117, 122 f., 178, 181, 183
- ethics and, 147
- Fall of, 79
- freedom of, 69, 146, 148
- mortality of, 100, 169

Manichaeanism, 31
Marxism, 148, 150, 154, 157 f., 173
Materialism, 135
Metaphysics, 65, 103
Ministry, 21, 59, 165
Missions, 27, 103 f., 138, 148, 173
Mohammedanism, 31
Monarchianism, 91 ff.
Monasticism, 84

Nationalism, 20, 48, 74, 135, 145
Nature, 29, 67, 105, 106 ff., 119, 134, 152
Nihilism, 107, 108 ff., 116 ff., 122, 137 ff., 181
Non-Church movement, 17 ff., 20, 46, 50, 58 f., 94, 124 ff., 137, 145, 163 ff., 170 f.
- ethics and, 21, 145, 149 ff.

Ontology, 67, 103, 156, 160 f.
- *Hāyā*tology and, 155

Pain, 123, 175
- as symbol, 76, 81 f., 96

Patripassianism, 76, 92 f., 176
Phenomenology, 49, 167
Philosophy, 101, 124, 127, 129 f., 133
- Japanese, 75, 102 f., 107, 119, 138, 146 f., 157 ff., 178
- of religion, 102 ff., 129 ff., 132

Pietism, 148, 150
Plymouth Brethren, 38
Prayer, 98, 120 f.
Predestination, 63 f., 66
Providence, 69

Reason, 128, 131
Reconciliation, 80, 97 f.

Religions, 14, 55, 136 f., 140, 181
Resurrection, 54, 123 f.
Revelation, 51 f., 56, 116, 122, 129 f., 134
  general, 127
Roman Catholicism, 26 f., 40, 50, 57 f., 60 ff., 143

Sacraments, 21, 24 f., 59, 165, 172
Salvation, 30, 37, 69, 89, 93, 122, 150. *See also* Anthropology
Sanctification, 37, 58, 63
Scholasticism, 133
Science, 67
Shintoism, 119, 136, 153
Sin, 29, 53, 69, 92, 98, 173. *See also* Anthropology
  punishment of, 81
Subjectivism, 59, 62, 147, 156
Subjectivity, 33 f., 58
Suffering, 74 ff., 87, 145, 172, 176
  justification of, 82 f.
Suicide, 53, 108 f., 138
Symbol, 101, 111, 121, 123, 129 f., 172, 180. *See also* Pain

Temporality, 106 ff., 112
Theologia crucis, 77
Theology, 71
  dialectical, 39, 55, 70, 130 ff., 145 ff., 172
  dogmatic, 63, 88 ff., 99
  experiential, 65, 68, 89
  hermeneutical interpretation of, 76, 89
  imitative, 13 f., 63
  indigenous, 18, 48, 50, 83 ff., 133 ff., 155
  as logos, 88 f.
  maturity of, 21, 62, 126 ff.
  modern, 68, 75, 80, 92. *See also* Liberalism
  natural, 127, 130, 142, 171
  as pathos, 88 f.
Time, 47, 70, 100 ff., 154
  direction of, 108, 112, 116, 160
  modes of, 106 ff., 111, 156, 159
Tradition, 14, 31, 37, 40, 50, 57, 62, 68, 74, 87, 124 f., 161, 170
  dualistic view of, 56 ff., 59, 64
  evangelical view of, 57, 60
Tragedy, 70, 113, 138
  Greek and Japanese, 86 ff.
Trinity, 59, 63 ff., 77, 90 ff., 93, 175

Waggishness, 141 f.
Wesleyanism, 20, 38
World, 29, 51, 71, 83, 112, 124, 138, 143, 161. *See also* Culture
  historical, 70

INDEX II

Japanese Terms

(*Not including words appearing in book titles*)

Akita, 140

Botsuga, 120
Bunka, 110
Bunretsu, 93
Bushidō, 140 f.

Denshō, 40, 56 ff., 62, 180
Dentō, 56 ff., 62, 180

Furoshiki, 74 f., 80

Gedatsu, 113
Genkan, 151
Geta, 17

Haiku, 73, 139
Hannja, 19
Harakiri, 138
Hyōkin, 141 f.

Iki, 139 ff.
Itsukushimi, 121

Kami-kaze, 140
Kijun, 40
Kyakubiki, 143
Kyochi, 120
Kyōdan, 23, 35, 77, 137

Mirai, 107, 115, 184
Mukyōkai, 18 ff., 27 f.

Nai-kyōkai, 19
Ningen, 147, 182

Reki-shi, 52
Rinri, 147

Sankō, 40
Seisho, 40
Seiten, 40
Shōrai, 107 ff., 115, 177, 184
Shukan-sei, 158
Shukanteki, 33 f., 156
Shutai, 34, 55, 158
Shutai-sei, 40, 158
Shutaiteki, 33 f., 62

Tsurasa, 86

Yabo, 139 ff.
Yukusue, 177